THE OLD-FASHIONED
DUTCH OVEN COOKBOOK

The Old-Fashioned

DUTCH OVEN
COOKBOOK

Complete with Authentic Sourdough Baking, Smoking
Fish and Game, Making Jerky, Pemmican, and
Other Lost Campfire Arts

By

DON HOLM
Author of *Reunion Summer*

COVER PLATE BY CHARLES CONKLING

Sketches by Jack Ostergren
The Oregon Journal

The CAXTON PRINTERS, Ltd.
CALDWELL, IDAHO
1975

First printing October, 1969
Second printing February, 1970
Third printing December, 1970
Fourth printing October, 1971
Fifth printing July, 1972
Sixth printing August, 1973
Seventh printing April, 1975

Standard Book Number 87004-133-9

Library of Congress Catalog Card Number 70-84782

Printed and bound in the United States of America by
The CAXTON PRINTERS, Ltd.
Caldwell, Idaho 83605
125763

To camp cooks everywhere!

Some excerpts in this volume were published first in the *Oregonian* and the *Sunday Oregonian* (Portland)

FOREWORD

ALTHOUGH I am not a cook of any merit—campfire or otherwise— for many years the idea for an authentic source of old-time, camp, trail, chuck-wagon, and pioneer-type recipes and methods, has nagged me.

It bothered me that, in these days of mechanical refrigeration, and new methods of preserving foods such as freeze drying, we were gradually losing many of the old arts—and particularly those used on the frontiers of young America, where a man lived close to nature and had to depend upon his own resources and ingenuity for survival.

Unfortunately, many of these old campfire arts were simply handed down orally. A long search through libraries and musty old books and journals failed to turn up any reliable sources. That's when I began collecting—first by writing down what I could remember out of my boyhood on the prairies of North Dakota, and from the years spent in the logging and mining camps and fishing villages of the West Coast and Alaska; and then by gathering material from other people and sources.

Once, when I asked John Jobson, camping editor of *Sports Afield*, for some information and advice based on his experiences, he kindly responded, but added that if I were attempting to write a book about Dutch ovens, I had more guts than he had!

Many people have contributed to this effort, some because of the nostalgic appeal of the subject itself, others because they wanted to see preserved in print many things that would otherwise be lost.

I am especially indebted to my bride Myrtle, an "authentic North Dakota farm gal," who assisted with the book and personally tested many of the recipes.

DON HOLM
BEAVERTON, OREGON
February, 1969

CONTENTS

THE OLD-FASHIONED
DUTCH OVEN COOKBOOK

INTRODUCTION

ON A GLOOMY November day in 1813, in a log cabin on the Missouri frontier near where Dundee now stands, a man named John Colter died of "jaundice." With him at the time were his bride Sally and a couple of neighbors.

Possibly one of these neighbors was old Dan'l Boone, then in his eighties, who lived nearby.

Colter, you may recall, was a veteran of the Lewis and Clark expedition who chose to remain in the Rockies, and went on to discover "Colter's Hell" and what is now Yellowstone National Park.

He was also America's first "Mountain Man," that unique breed of wild adventurers who roamed the mountains for thirty or forty years and opened the Far West for the latecomers.

For the purpose of this tale, however, it is only pertinent to point out that the sale bill of Colter's personal property, as listed by his executor contained the following item:

"To John Simpson—one Dutch oven—$4.00."

By this time the Dutch oven had already been part of frontier history and legend for more than one hundred years. It is also interesting to note that in 1813 Colter's oven brought the equivalent of a week's pay at the executor's auction. Today you can buy an identical Dutch oven for about the same price, but it represents only an hour's work for many wage earners.

One of the most efficient cooking devices ever developed, the Dutch oven evolved out of necessity, as do many practical inventions. In pre-Revolutionary days, when the American frontier was still within sight of the Eastern tidewater, life was simple, conveniences few, and most activities were "outdoor" experiences.

Indeed, in those days most kitchens were "outdoors" —or in separate buildings or shanty houses.

As the frontier moved westward, settlers developed a mobile society and a tradition for practical innovation that helped shape this nation for the next three hundred years.

This constant packing up, starting life over again on the frontier to the west, encouraged such innovations as the Kentucky rifle (actually developed in Lancaster, Pennsylvania), and the Conestoga wagon. A family pushing through the Cumberland Gap and into the raw wilderness of the Old Northwest, had to limit baggage to essentials, and to evolve equipment that was versatile and dependable.

The Dutch oven was one of these—readily portable, amazingly simple and versatile, and it eliminates the need for a bulky stove or even a fireplace.

Before the introduction of ironware and copper kettles, the Indians cooked almost all their food in tightly woven baskets filled with water into which they dropped rocks heated in the campfire. The Dutch oven was designed to be placed directly into the coals of an open fire.

It didn't take frontier cooks long to find out that with this gadget they could bake bread and biscuits, boil potatoes and other vegetables, fry fish, bacon and eggs, make deep-dish pies, and fix the best doggone stew you ever tasted.

Frontiersmen discovered that by placing a cup of water in the bottom, all kinds of meat, fish, and fowl could be roasted to perfection with little or no attention.

Foods could be fried easily and conveniently in lard or bear grease in the pot or on the inverted lid.

The Dutch oven was also ideal for baking pies, biscuits, cookies, and even cakes either directly in the bottom of the pot or on flat rocks placed inside baking pans on top of these.

Stews could be cooked any old way—on top of the fire or with the oven buried in the coals. You could throw almost anything into the pot except a buffalo hide or a cast-off saddle, and come up with mulligan ambrosia.

Frontier cooks also learned to heap coals on top of the lid to improve its roasting and baking qualities. Later models were then cast with a turned-up flange around the edge of the lid to hold the coals.

The standard pattern for the Dutch oven was said to have been perfected by that imaginative craftsman, Paul Revere. His version was almost identical to those manufactured today, although some of his models were equipped with a detachable frying pan type handle.

The manufacture of the kettle was common in colonial New England. Traders from Holland bought large quantities for barter with the Indians and the frontier settlers. This is how the utensil came to be known as the "Dutch" oven.

The Dutch oven went with the westering land seekers who pushed their wagons and packtrains through the Dark and Bloody Ground, or floated down the Ohio on flatboats, as did the family of Captain William Clark who years later was to join Meriwether Lewis in their epic adventure.

Westward again went the Dutch oven, to the Mississippi and beyond, across the wide Missouri and up to its very source, over the Continental Divide to the old South Sea, which we now call the Pacific. It went across the plains to Santa Fe, to the Canadian frontier, and northward to Alaska and the Yukon.

The early explorers, the military expeditions, the trappers and fur traders, the first sodbusters—all depended upon the Dutch oven.

The oven spread over the plains with the cattlemen, into the high mountain meadows with the sheepherders. And it is still used extensively today by ranchers, herders, packers, and outfitters.

The Dutch oven, in addition to filling men's bellies, also inspired untold numbers of place names on the maps today. In Lane County, Oregon, for example, on the South Fork of the McKenzie River, there is a place called Dutch Oven Camp. It got its name when a burro fell over a cliff at this point and was killed. The only part of the pack undamaged was a demijohn of whiskey.

Characteristically, the party rather than rejoicing over this, bemoaned the loss of their Dutch oven, which was broken. For many years the broken pieces remained on the site in memory of this "tragedy."

In the 1850's that mysterious race, the Basques, began arriving in the American West as immigrants from their ancient homeland in the mountains on the border of France and Spain. They brought with them their knowledge of sheep and love for the wide-open country, and settled in the remote sections of Oregon, Washington, Idaho, Nevada, Colorado, Arizona, and Wyoming.

Today their descendants number more than sixty thousand and many have left the mountains and deserts to become successful businessmen, doctors, lawyers, and professionals of all kinds.

One thing they did not bring to America with them, however, was the Dutch oven. They adapted it to their camp life. In fact, they became so expert in the use of the Dutch oven that it became part of their tradition and customs.

One of the most heavenly experiences a hungry outdoor traveler can enjoy is happening upon a Basque sheepherder's wagon as he is digging out a Dutch oven filled with crusty, golden-brown sourdough bread with its heady aroma wafting across the desert.

For breadmaking the Basques used a huge Dutch oven which, when the cover was removed, left a loaf engraved with every line, ring, and symbol cast in the metal. Many Basques would scratch each loaf with the sign of the Cross before cutting it.

Basque herders, out on the range, rose at dawn, crawled out of their canvas bags, dashed cold water in their faces, and sat down to a breakfast of scalding coffee mixed with canned cow and munched on crusts of this sourdough bread. This held them until midday when the main meal was served, usually an omelet of eggs, bacon, and potatoes, washed down with a strong wine from a goatskin *bota*.

Today the Dutch oven—or perhaps more properly the "camp Dutch oven," to distinguish it from some of these modern abominations that are merchandised as Dutch ovens—is still practical for any situation where weight is not a problem (and some of the new aluminum models promise to solve this), such as on camping and pack trips, in backyard cookouts, in the family room fireplace, and anywhere that open fires are not objectionable or prohibited.

One thing is certain: No one has ever been able to improve upon its cooking qualities, whether it's called a Dutch oven, camp Dutch oven, Western Dutch oven, country oven, or chuck-wagon pot.

It's truly a culinary dream machine that can make the clumsiest tenderfoot look like a cow-country *escoffier*.

And, because its use is so closely related to many

other traditional Western or country-style culinary arts, we've also included in this volume sections on sourdough, jerky, pemmican, wild game, and a whole chuck-wagon box full of campfire goodies.

I

THE CARE AND FEEDING OF A CAMP DUTCH OVEN

TODAY THE camp Dutch oven is not regularly stocked by supermarkets and hardware stores, although some of the better sporting goods or "outdoor" shops display it. Usually it must be ordered directly from the manufacturer or jobber.

Once one is acquired, however, guard it with your life. Above all, do not loan it out, especially to a friend

or relative, for like books (possibly even this one), real Dutch ovens are never returned.

Assuming that you have not already purchased, borrowed, snitched, or otherwise acquired a camp Dutch oven, let us proceed with a description. First, a warning: When purchasing one, be not misled by some smart-alec clerk in a department-store cookware section. Do not let him pass off on you one of those "home" Dutch ovens which are simply flat-bottomed kettles with self-basting covers made for kitchen cooking only.

The camp Dutch oven is made specifically for open-fire cooking. It is made of heavy, cast iron or aluminum in basic sizes from eight inches to sixteen inches in diameter, and from four to six inches deep.

It's heavy, thick, and flat on the bottom, and has three short legs which protrude about two inches, like a stubby tripod. The pot is fitted with a bail. The lid is cast of the same heavy metal and is tight-fitting and slightly domed in the center, with a handle in the middle of the dome. On the underside of the center handle there is often a shallow notch which is the exact balance point for picking up the lid with a hook or poker. The rim of the lid is flanged for the purpose of holding hot coals.

One of the secrets of a good camp Dutch oven is the proper "seasoning" of the metal. New cast-iron ovens *must* be seasoned before using, and if the cook or dishwasher uses strong modern detergents in cleaning, it probably will have to be reseasoned all over again.

In olden days the porous ironware was coated with a varnish or lacquer to prevent rusting. This had to be burned off or removed by scrubbing. Modern ovens are coated with a waxlike preservative that needs only a good washing in hot, sudsy water, followed by a good rinsing and drying. They still have to be cured before cooking with them. Do not omit this step.

Some cooks prefer to deep fry with the oven the first time or two. The simplest way is to boil grease, suet, or lard, spreading it thoroughly—not forgetting the underside of the lid—with a swab (which can be made in camp with a stick and a clean rag wrapped around the end). For this the oven can be heated right inside your kitchen oven. When the grease starts to smoke, remove the oven from the heat and wipe it out thoroughly, but leave a thin coating.

Deep-frying fish, donuts, or chicken the first few times will accomplish the same result.

Whenever the utensil is removed from the heat, always take the cover off immediately to prevent excessive moisture from dripping into the food. Most cooks grease the ironware after every use to prevent water and chemicals from coming in contact with the metal. Don't over-do this cleaning process or you may have to reseason the pot. Do not use strong detergents or scour with a cleaning pad.

With normal care and use a good camp Dutch oven will last several lifetimes and get "sweeter" each time it's used.

The aluminum version of the camp Dutch oven is a new development and at this writing largely untried and unnoticed by professional cooks, columnists, outdoor writers and editors, and sportsmen's groups.

It is, however, worth your consideration. Manufactured by one or two U.S. firms, it is one-third the weight of cast iron, and thus more easily portable on camping trips. We have used our two models for several years with excellent results. The aluminum oven is durable and rustproof. It has no metal flavor pick-up and requires no breaking in. Our experience with it indicates, though, that it should be seasoned the same as the cast-iron version. It is important that you do not overheat an aluminum oven.

One of the aluminum models has a detachable three-legged grill which not only provides a base for a ten-inch oven but by itself is a handy support for cooking pots and frying pans.

Aluminum ovens can be used with wood fires and also with charcoal briquets. When using charcoal or wood coals be careful not to get it too hot. An excess of heat on the lid or under the oven could not only burn the food but cause *permanent damage to the oven.* Usually not more than ten to twelve briquets or coals, below and fifteen to eighteen on the lid, evenly distributed, are enough for the twelve-inch size. The intensity of the heat can be regulated by mixing ashes with the coals.

The camp Dutch oven, either iron or aluminum, can be permanently damaged by pouring cold water into a hot oven, or uneven heating such as putting only half the oven or lid on the coals, by careless packing while traveling (the legs can be broken off or pushed up through the bottom by too much jostling), and by rust and corrosion.

The lid, turned upside down on the coals or on the pot, can be used for frying eggs, bacon, or grilling hot cakes. When using more than one oven, the second can be stacked on top of the first without the necessity of spreading more coals on the ground.

One should probably call the aluminum model the *contemporary* Dutch oven, which has some advantages and some disadvantages when compared with the traditional cast-iron model. The aluminum model is the only one that can be backpacked by a hiker. It costs about the same as the ironware. But it has a much lower fuel requirement, which can lead to trouble. The trick is to use from one half to two-thirds less fuel or heat to start with and control the heat more carefully.

The old camp Dutch oven evolved through centuries of experience. It was designed for cooking complete meals on open fires without the need for other appliances. (A shovel, pothook, and grease swab come in handy, though.) Its thick construction distributes the heat evenly and thoroughly from a small bed of coals assisted by the tight-fitting, flanged lid.

It can be hung over an open fire, set down in the fire, or buried in a pit of coals. It is at once a kettle, a frying pan, an oven, a pot, and even a stove, all in one portable utensil.

On a camping or hunting trip you can prepare a roast or stew, or even sheepherder bread, go away for a half day or so, only to return bone-tired and happily find a rib-sticking meal waiting for chow down.

No cooking device has ever been invented which can produce such delicious, nutritious, and delectable meals with so little trouble and skill. Even the most inept dude can whip up thick stews, pot roasts, steaks, chowders, baked beans, chili, bread, biscuits, cakes, pies, and even French fried potatoes unsurpassed.

The recipes following involve the two basic methods of Dutch-oven cookery—above ground and below ground. Generally the above-ground method is best for fast meals, and below ground for leisurely cooking while you are doing something else, such as pitching a Muddler Minnow at a brown trout in a nearby stream, or following the trail of an elk up a remote canyon.

II

IT'S EASY THE DUTCH OVEN WAY

I LEAVE IT to the headshrinkers to explain why a person's taste buds are so closely coupled to nostalgia. It's hard to find a person over forty who doesn't remember, with varying degrees of longing, Mother's lemon pie; or her homemade bread hot and crispy from the oven,

swathed in butter and honey; or perhaps her special way of preparing scalloped corn.

Such memories, of course, are wonderful, and a man without them is less than a whole man; but I'm just as sure that Mom, herself, has no hankerin' to go back to the good old days of cranky wood ranges, water heated in kettles, hot kitchens on hot summer days, outdoor plumbing, no refrigeration. No normal person, I'm sure, wants to trade his Ferrari for a horse and buggy, or go back to kerosene lighting, castor-oil remedies, and Chic Sales—not when we have electricity, instant communications, jet transportation, and advanced scientific and medical techniques.

Just the same, not all change is for the better, or all modern innovations necessarily improvements. The so-called patio barbecue or backyard cookout, for example, can only be described as a reversion to the cooking habits of the Folsom man. The gorgeous color photos (carefully posed) in some women's magazines notwithstanding, this form of cookery can only be called barbaric. Nothing ruins good food, not to mention tender digestive tracts, so quickly as the open combustion of charcoal and other coal tar and petroleum derivatives. And never have so many otherwise intelligent and discriminating people been conned into such a half-baked ritual as by the so-called "patio cookout."

Which only proves that when it comes to fads, Joe Citizen usually gets what he lets someone else talk him into—including heartburn and a new longing for Mother's old favorite dishes.

But the old-fashioned camp Dutch oven—which is neither an oven nor an invention of the Dutch—is one appliance which may yet save the suburban stomach from the perils of modern tribal rites. Moreover, it's fun, once in a while, to get lost in yesterday.

Virtually any dish is easy for the Dutch-oven cook, from baking to broiling, roasting, frying, stewing, and deep frying. If there is anything that can't be cooked in a Dutch oven, I don't know what it is. But baking and roasting are where it comes into its own. Minor errors have little effect on quality, and nothing is easier for the beginner to learn on.

The basic method for pot roasts calls for a preheated oven and lid to prevent heat from being drawn out of the porous iron by cold ingredients. Then a chunk of suet is dropped in and heated until it begins to smoke. The roast is immediately seared on all sides, salted, and a cup of hot water eased in. When the lid is put on, the roast will then be self-basting.

The next step is the addition of vegetables such as turnips, carrots, potatoes, onions, parsnips, garlic, and what have you. Some cooks leave them out until an hour or so before serving. It's more convenient, though, and usually okay, to dump them all in right away so that the whole meal is under preparation at once. The pot roast then requires no more attention until all hands return from afield. Moderate heat should be used in this case to prevent the vegetables from mushing.

Wild game is best cooked by the Dutch-oven pan-roasting method. Even the toughest cuts of meat can be made tender this way. The secret is in the slow cooking and simmering after the initial browning or searing.

For hole-in-the-ground cooking, dig a pit larger and deeper than the camp Dutch oven. Line it with small stones or aluminum foil to prevent loss of heat through the ground. (Be sure to select a site that is pure mineral soil and not full of humus, or you may be the cause of a forest or range fire, which will make you extremely unpopular in most parts, podner.) Build a fire in the hole and let it burn briskly an hour or so, or until there is nothing left but hot coals. Remove some of these, place oven in pit with the rest, and rake the coals back over the oven.

Cover the whole ball of wax with fresh dirt in a blanket about four inches thick. Most dishes require from four to eight hours cooking in this way. The cooking can be hurried along by building another fire on top of the dirt.

Bean Hole Beans

1 lb. navy or pea beans	½ cup molasses
1 tsp. salt	2 chunks of bacon
pepper	

Soak beans overnight, then bring to a boil and cook until skins burst when spooned and blown. Pour off liquid and save. Drop a chunk of salt pork into Dutch oven, pour in beans; add salt, molasses, and some fresh-ground pepper to bean water, then pour over beans to cover and add another chunk of pork on top. Put on lid and set in fire pit, using hole-in-ground method.

Camp Chowder

Start with diced pork or bacon and cook onions and potatoes in it. Then add fish and vegetables, canned or dried milk. Cook like bean hole beans. You may want to start an argument over milk versus tomato sauce in chowder, but I like it both ways. Use your own proportions of ingredients. A little ingenuity here goes a long way.

Camp Scrounger

Cook as a stew the following, or a reasonable fac-
simile: Beef shank bone, venison or bear or elk or woodchuck, stewing hen, potatoes, turnips, carrots, celery,
pureed tomatoes, green beans, shelled peas, sweet
corn, shredded cabbage, okra, chopped parsley, celery
leaves, red peppers, bell peppers, rosemary or thyme,
ground black pepper.

To each quart of water, use enough to cover meat,
add one tablespoon of salt, bring to a boil, then cook
slowly until tender. Remove meat and cut into bite-size
chunks and replace in pot. Bring to a boil and add the
above vegetables. When liquid comes to a rolling boil,
add condiments, reduce heat, and cook slowly until
done.

Prairie Pea Soup

During the Dust Bowl days I lived on this recipe for
one entire winter—and by spring couldn't look a pea
in the eye without groaning. A few months later,
though, after a change of diet, I was ready for it again.

2 cups split peas	¼ lb. diced salt pork
1 large onion	salt and pepper
1½ cups water	

Fry salt pork until crisp. Saute onion (diced) in the
drippings, drain and put pork, onion, and peas in pot.
Cover with water and simmer for about four hours,
replacing water as needed, stirring frequently. Season
with salt and pepper. Soup should be thick as cream
when dished up to hungry hands.

Basque Chicken

I took this recipe off a grizzled old hombre in the remote mountain country around the ghost town of Silver

City east of Jordan Valley years ago. He didn't put up much of a struggle. You wouldn't either after stuffing yourself on this dish served with garlic croutons.

Boil or steam a stewing hen until tender. Separate the meat from the bones and chop up. Strain broth and skim off fat. Use this fat to mix a paste, then add this to the simmering broth until it is as thick as a light cream. Season to taste with salt and pepper. Just before serving add chopped chicken, pimento, and cooked green peppers.

Dutch Oven Pot Roast

At breakfast time, with as much foresight as you can muster early in the morning, braise a roast of a size to fit your Dutch oven, and place in the pot with one-half cup warm water, some carrots, potatoes, onions, garlic and cloves, salt and pepper, and perhaps a half package of dried onion soup. A can of consomme can be used instead of water. Be sure to leave a space between the lid and the top of the meat.

When the campfire has burned down, shovel some of the coals aside and place the Dutch oven in the fire pit. Cover the lid with coals and bury completely with fresh dirt.

When you return at night, your dinner will be waiting for you—and you'll be ready for it.

Dutch Oven Stew

Prepare same as above, except that the meat is cut into chunks before placing in pot and the water or liquid should be enough to cover the meat.

With all pot roasts, make gravy out of the liquid stock in the bottom of the pot, and season to taste. Pot

roasts as well as stews are best served with hot sourdough or French bread.

The One Shot Pot

This is for the guy who's been chosen to stay in camp
as cook for the day, but who hasn't had much experience—and maybe is a little lazy.

Place three or four pounds of boiling beef in the
Dutch oven with enough cold water to cover. Bring to
a boil and let it bubble for a couple of hours. Add carrots, parsnips, turnips, and any other fresh, tame, or
wild vegetables at hand, and cook some more. Then
add the potatoes to complete the dinner and simmer
until done.

Just before serving make dumplings out of prepared
biscuit mix and drop into the bubbling, savory liquid
in which the meat and vegetables have been cooking all
day. Feed a meal like this to a bunch of tired and
growling hunters when they get back to camp wet and
hungry, and you'll draw permanent duty as camp chef.

Deep Fat Frying

Potatoes, onions, fish, steak, chops, as well as fritters
and donuts, can be cooked in the camp Dutch oven by
the deep fat method. The oven should be preheated on
coals and beef suet, cooking oil, or bacon fat heated until boiling. The grease should be hot enough so that
when a cube of dry bread is tossed into the fat, it be-
comes golden brown in about a minute. The grease at
this temperature will be sending up delicate wisps of
smoke, but not smoking over the entire surface.

Ease the food chunks to be fried into the hot grease
carefully, one at a time, removing when thoroughly

cooked. Use pieces as small as possible and do not load pot with too many as otherwise it will lower the temperature of the grease too fast.

Mouse River Chili Con Carne

Years ago, as a nineteen-year-old lad roamin' around the world, I worked a spell for a man who had retired after making a fortune with a chain of lunch counters down on the Texican border. Even retired, he could not help looking for good dishes. This was one of them, which I copied down on the back of the first Social Security card the New Deal issued me. It's the best chili I've ever tasted before or since.

¼ cup cubed beef suet	1 clove garlic
1 lb. ground round or chuck	1 tbsp. chili powder
⅛ cup olive oil	1 tsp. paprika
½ cup chopped onions	1 tbsp. salt
1 tbsp. oregano	1 small red pepper crushed
1 cup hot water	fresh ground black pepper

Put into Dutch oven the suet, ground meat, and olive oil. Cook until meat is brown. To this add chopped onions, garlic, chili powder, paprika, salt and pepper, red pepper, oregano, and water, cooking about three minutes while stirring well. Simmer until done.

If you like *frijoles con chili con carne*, add a small can of pureed tomatoes to pot and dish up over cooked kidney beans.

Only a peasant would mix beans into a chili pot.

Dutch Oven Steak

Preheat oven and grease with two large tablespoons of fat or suet. Meanwhile pound flour into a round steak, about a half cup per pound of meat. Sear the steak and a sliced onion in the hot grease. Season with salt and pepper. Cover steak with hot water or a couple cups of pureed tomatoes and cook slowly for about two hours.

Pepper Steaks

For each person cut one-half pound of flank steak against the grain and about one-fourth-inch-thick slices. Peel and slice an onion. Quarter one medium-size green pepper, remove seeds, and cut into half-inch strips. Melt 1 tablespoon of shortening or bacon fat in oven. Fry onions until brown. Add meat slices and brown. Put in pepper slices and cover oven with lid. Heap coals on top of lid. Cook until meat is tender. Season to taste.

Baked Turkey

Dredge a small disjointed turkey in well-seasoned flour (shake up in a paper bag), and brown in bacon fat. Use a large enough Dutch oven to handle the bird. Add a little hot water, put on lid and cover with coals, banking hot coals around the oven. Cook for two to four hours, depending upon the size of the bird, adding small amounts of hot water occasionally if necessary.

Old-fashioned Potato Soup

This is the way the farm gals used to make it in North Dakota when a blizzard was blowing outside and the pantry was getting low on grub.

Cook ½ cup navy beans and 4 large diced potatoes separately. When done put in pot with 2 small sliced onions, salt and pepper, and add enough milk to make as thin as desired—but not too thin. Add a big chunk of butter just before serving.

This also works fine with a camp Dutch oven and tastes even better cooked outdoors, summer or winter, if that's possible.

Chuck-wagon Tongue

Wash well a 3-pound fresh or smoked tongue. Cover with hot water, add 2 teaspoons salt, 2 or 3 bay leaves, 6 whole allspices, 3 whole black peppers, 1 onion sliced, 1 carrot, and 1 celery stalk. Simmer but do not boil for 3 hours and let cool in its own juice. For snacks and sandwiches.

Have a Heart

Wash a beef (or big game) heart well and cut into small squares. Stew for 10 minutes in enough water to draw out blood. Skim, take out meat, and strain liquid. Return meat to the liquid, add seasonings, simmer until tender. Make a brown gravy of the juice.

Spanish Rice

This is one Mom used to make, adapted to the camp Dutch oven.

4 tbsp. suet	1 cup brown or white rice
1 small chopped onion	3 cups tomatoes
1 lb. raw hamburger	¼ tsp. pepper
1½ cups boiling water	2½ tsp. salt

Melt suet or fat in preheated oven. Add onion, hamburger, and brown in hot fat. Add rice, tomatoes, salt and pepper, and boiling water. Cover and simmer for 1½ hours or until rice is tender.

Suet Pudding

Mix 1 cup chopped suet, 3½ cups flour, 2 cups raisins, 1 cup currants, 2 teaspoons soda, 1 cup molasses, and 1 cup sour milk, and steam in Dutch oven for 2 hours with lid on.

Parched Corn

How do you suppose the *voyageurs* paddled Hudson's Bay Company freight canoes all the way from Montreal to Fort Vancouver, packing most of their rations with them? They practically lived on parched corn.

Preheat Dutch oven on hot coals. Do not use water or grease. Drop in shelled sweet corn kernels and toast them, turning or stirring frequently to keep from burning. When corn is brown and crunchy it is done.

Like pemmican, parched corn is an ideal trail food, light and easily stored for long periods. It was a staple of the French-Canadians, the fur traders and mountain men, as well as Indian tribes like the Arikaras and Mandans.

Camp Rice

One of the most versatile of all trail foods, rice is light and easily packed. It is a wholesome substitute for potatoes. It is, however, seldom cooked properly. This is how it should be done:

Thoroughly clean and strain a cup of rice, rinsing often, and even rubbing it between your fingers. Heat water in Dutch oven or pot, enough to cover, and boil. The rice will expand many times. Add a little at a time when water is at a rolling boil, so that it never stops boiling. Cook uncovered until the grains are tender and fluffy. Drain and rinse in hot water and let dry in a warm place.

Serve with tomato sauce or gravy, with melted butter and sugar or salt; or as cereal with milk and sugar.

Camp Bacon

This is how to cook large quantities of bacon for half-starved hunters or fishermen who can't wait for the slow four-slices-at-a-time process on the griddle:

Slice bacon and drop in camp Dutch oven. You don't even have to bother with separating the slices and you can cook several pounds at a time this way. Stir constantly with a long-handled fork until bacon is done to proper color and crispness.

Dutch Oven Potatoes

Fry ½ pound of salt pork in open oven or pan until crisp. Remove the pork and fry 4 medium-size onions diced in grease until soft. Dice 8 medium-size potatoes and add to onion. Cook in covered oven until done. Remove the cover and brown. Add the salt pork which has meanwhile been chopped fine. Do not stir. Turn when brown on bottom. Salt and pepper to taste.

Camp Puffs

Stir together 2 cups of cold mashed potatoes, 1 cup milk, 2 well-beaten eggs, 1 tablespoon melted butter. Bake in preheated oven like biscuits.

For a special treat, and I do mean special, mix deviled ham and chopped onions into batter.

Chuck-wagon Dumplings

Here is the basic recipe for dumplings that will enhance your newly-acquired reputation as camp cook.

Mix 1 cup flour, 2 teaspoons baking powder, 1 teaspoon salt, 2 tablespoons of shortening, with enough milk to make a soft dough. Drop by spoonfuls in boiling pot of roast or stew.

Camp Coffee

In a pinch your Dutch oven can be used for making coffee. Break 1 egg, crushing shell, mix with ½ cup coffee and ½ cup water, adding to pot with 4 cups boiling water and stir. Bring to a boil. Let stand for 5 minutes, then add ½ cup cold water.

Of course, if you want to make coffee this way in a regular pot it's okay, too.

Do It Yourself Piecrust

2½ cups flour   ¾ cup shortening
1 tsp. salt   ¼ cup cold water

Mix salt into flour and break shortening to pea-size, then sprinkle water on mixture until dough can be formed into ball. You can also use a commercial mix.

For a deep-dish Dutch oven pie, roll out dough ⅛ inch thick and 8 inches wider than oven. Fold once and lay in cold oven. Then unfold and tuck into shape, being careful not to stretch. Bake shell in oven for about 10 minutes. The shell should feel firm but not done. Rub bottom with margarine, then add a prepared fruit pie filling or fresh fruit, being careful not to break crust.

With a second rolled-out crust cover the pie completely or make a lattice-type top crust. Replace lid and bake until crust is brown. Prepared fillings don't need cooking, but raw fresh fruit requires baking entire pie at the same time, starting with a cold oven. Don't forget to make steam vents.

The trick is to get the oven just the right heat—not too hot and not too cool. Check progress often with tongs or hook. While Dutch ovens were designed for one-pot meals, there is no reason why several ovens, in different sizes, can't be used—one for meat, one for vegetables, or bread, or pies, or what-have-you.

Dutch Oven Apples

Wash and core six or eight large apples. Fill holes with sugar, raisins and butter pat, plus cinnamon if desired. Put apples on a greased pie tin with a small amount of water. Place tin in oven on legs made of pebbles or bottle caps to prevent scorching. Cover and bake for about thirty minutes.

Foiled Potatoes

Scrub half a dozen or so big potatoes. Prick skin with knife and grease. Wrap each individually in foil and put on a pie tin. Set pie tin on pebbles or bottle caps inside preheated Dutch oven. Cover and pile coals on lid. Bake at least an hour. Test with a sharp splinter. Add butter and salt to taste when done.

III

BY BREAD ALONE

WANT TO BE top hand on an *expedition* (as well as around home)?

Then learn the basic baking techniques with a camp Dutch oven.

Besides, there's no better way to bake biscuits or bread, above ground or below. Here's the way it's done:

First: Preheat the oven and lid thoroughly. If anything, the lid should be hotter than the oven. Have plenty of live coals and some means of controlling the heat such as a shovel or pothook for raking coals and lifting oven and lid.

Second: Prepare the dough and have it ready to drop in.

Third: Grease oven, dropping in a chunk of fat or suet, swabbing it around with a piece of cloth on a green stick.

Fourth: Break off chunks of dough and drop in the hot grease. When brown on the bottom, turn over and set the lid on the oven. Shovel hot coals away from the main fire, set oven on this and pile coals on top of lid. The coals should be gray in color.

After about ten minutes the biscuits should have a delicious golden look. If not, add more coals. If burned the first time, use less heat. You will learn by experience to judge the proper time without a second thought.

Remember that for baking, the oven *and* lid should be preheated in order to prevent bottom scorching and uneven cooking.

This method can also be used for pies (using a pie pan, of course), cakes, corn pone, bannock or sourdough biscuits. Hot cakes can be cooked on the bottom of the oven, or on the upside down lid, if no griddle is available (or on the flat part of an old shovel in a pinch).

Bread takes longer and should be baked underground, preferably starting in the morning. When the fire pit is full of hot coals, shovel out about half and set the preheated and greased oven in the hole. Of course, you have already put the bulging, raised chunk of dough into the oven. Now cover the lid and shovel the rest of the embers and ashes on top, leaving the bail sticking out. Cover with dirt and forget it for three to four hours.

Remember that sourdough requires a hotter fire and a longer cooking time than ordinary dough (see chapter on sourdough cookery).

Basic Camp Baking Mix

1 cup flour	¼ tsp. salt
1 round tsp. baking powder	1 round tbsp. shortening
	1 tbsp. sugar

(For low altitudes, try using more baking powder.)

Melt the shortening in a small pan or container. Stir up dry ingredients with a fork to work air into the mix. Add just enough water to get the right consistency. Put the melted shortening into the water quickly so that it does not thicken or harden. The dough should be thicker than pancake batter, but not as thick as for drop biscuits. Milk can be used instead of water for the dough.

This recipe doubled will fill a twelve-inch Dutch oven.

Expedition Mix

Before leaving for the hills or woods, a basic baking mix can can be prepared as follows:

Mix 12 cups flour, 2 tablespoons salt, ¼ cup double-acting baking powder, and 1 pound shortening. Mix into a coarse texture and store until needed in refrigerator. Just before you leave, pack mix in 2- and 4-cup measurements into separate plastic bags.

Basic Biscuits

Add ½ cup water or reconstituted dried milk or canned cow to 2 cups of the expedition mix. Knead lightly and roll out ¾-inch thick cake on wax paper or foil. Cut into biscuit-size portions for baking in Dutch oven.

Or use the basic camp mix, tearing off chunks about the size of a heaping tablespoon.

When the Dutch oven starts to smoke lightly it is ready for biscuit dough. To test the lid, wet finger and tap metal lightly. If it sizzles, it's the right heat. Load the oven with biscuit chunks, making a ring around the outside, then filling in the center.

Place the lid on top and rotate to get a snug fit. Pile coals on top of lid.

If you can stand it for about five minutes, you are then permitted to take a peek by tipping up the lid with a pothook or tongs. If they have risen and are starting to brown, they are about right. If they are solid brown, the oven is too hot and the biscuits will burn before baked clean through. You can adjust the heat by allowing a little cold air in. If the tops look good but the bottoms are dark or burned, remove the oven from the bed of coals.

If everything is normal, and the heat at the proper degree, it will take about fifteen minutes to bake a batch. When ready set the oven to one side, break open a biscuit, drop on a slab of butter and some honey or jam, and you've taken your first step toward heaven.

After a session of baking the Dutch oven can be cleaned simply by wiping thoroughly with a paper towel while the metal is still warm. Then brush on a slight trace of fresh grease to prevent rust from forming. Do not use scouring pads or cleaning compounds.

Using the basic camp mix, you can also bake other tidbits. For coffee cake, just add sugar, butter, cinnamon, and some raisins to top of dough after it is in the oven.

Add an egg, a pinch of nutmeg for each cup of mix, and doubling the amount of sugar, you have a delicious cobbler dough or pancake batter—although for hot cakes you must add more liquid to make a thinner batter.

For corn bread use half cornmeal and half flour in the basic biscuit mix.

Biscuit Bread

For this simply spread dough mix in a well-greased Dutch oven without cutting into chunks. When the top is brown, turn carefully and brown the other side. Split and butter.

Scones

Stir 3 tablespoons of sugar into 2 cups of expedition baking mix with ½ cup of milk or water, and some raisins, huckleberries, or blueberries. Pat out and cut into pie-shaped wedges. Cook in Dutch oven with a small amount of grease. Turn when brown on one side.

Hermit Cakes

Stir 3 tablespoons of dried milk and one tablespoon of evaporated or fresh milk to 2 cups of baking mix to make a thin batter. Add a cup of blueberries, huckleberries, serviceberries, or lingonberries with a couple tablespoons of sugar for something special. Grill like hot cakes.

Corn Bread

Mix 1 cup cornmeal to 2 cups of expedition baking mix, with 2 eggs or equivalent, 1 cup buttermilk or 3 tablespoons dried buttermilk and 1 cup water. Add ½ teaspoon baking soda, ¼ cup melted bacon fat or butter. Bake in thin layers.

Camp Bread

Scald 2 cups of reconstituted dried milk or canned cow, mix 5 tablespoons of sugar and 1 tablespoon of salt, and set aside. Dissolve 2 packages of dried yeast in 2 cups of lukewarm water. Add to milk mixture. Then add 6 cups of flour and beat smooth, mixing in 5 tablespoons of melted bacon fat, or shortening, and enough flour to make easy kneading. Work until dough is smooth and elastic. Put in greased bowl or pot and allow to rise double. Divide into 4 loaves, place in greased pans, cover and allow to rise again until double. Bake over hot fire. (In kitchen use the equivalent of 425° for 15 minutes, then reduce heat to 375° for 30 minutes.)

Fried Bread

After the first rising of basic bread dough, tear off pieces about the size of walnuts and pull into flat shape. Fry in deep fat and sprinkle with powdered sugar.

Coffee Cake

Preheat oven and lid. Mix 1 cup self-rising cake flour, 2 tablespoons instant coffee, ¼ cup sugar. Stir in ½ cup of canned cow. Grease oven and pour in mixture. Cover and cook until bottom is firm and browned, about 10 minutes. Then turn cake over and brown the other side.

For cake flour you can substitute 1 cup of all-purpose flour, 1½ teaspoons baking powder, and ⅛ teaspoon salt, increasing milk to ¾ cup.

Sheepherder Bread

Basque herders in the remote high desert country of southeastern Oregon long ago devised what they called "big bread." Since a herder had to be away from the wagon all day (this wagon, by the way, was the forerunner of our modern pickup truck campers), he dug a two-foot hole in the ground and built a roaring fire in the morning, usually before daylight. When the fire burned down to coals, he prepared the bread dough. Then he loaded the oven, buried it in the coals, and shoveled a layer of dirt over the whole ball of wax. When he returned that night, there was the bread ready to eat and finger-lickin' good. Now you know why sheepherders enjoy their lonely life.

Dutch Oven Corn Bread

Mix 2 cups of cornmeal, 1 teaspoon salt, and 1½ cups milk or warm water. Drop into preheated and greased Dutch oven. Bake for 45 minutes. Let stand for a few minutes and it's ready to chomp on. For johnny cake use one beaten egg stirred in, decrease amount of liquid. Fry in hot greased oven.

Bannock Bill's Trail Biscuits

The measure of a man in the North Country was how well he could whip up a mess of bannock, or trail biscuits. Here's how old Bannock Bill out of Milepost X up in the Fraser country used to do it:

Mix 1 cup flour, 1 teaspoon baking soda, 1 tablespoon dried milk, 2 tablespoons cooking oil or shortening or bacon fat, ½ teaspoon salt. Add enough water to make a soft dough. Grease the Dutch oven or the lid and tilt up facing the coals; or put the cover on and bury in hot coals with more hot coals on lid. Cook slowly, being careful not to get the oven too hot or the biscuits will burn. The trick is to get them brown on the outside and well-cooked on the inside.

Most gents preferred "sweet bannock" because it added nourishment and energy to their trail diet. This was made by adding raisins and sugar to the dough while mixing.

Coffee and . . .

Donuts, sinkers, doughty cakes, fried cakes, quick bread—no matter what you call them, the donut is one of man's best friends and oldest treats, going back thousands of years, only to be discovered and rediscovered again and again with renewed delight.

Popular in England during the early sixteenth century, the idea was brought to America by Dutch and English colonists. Originally prepared as balls or nuts of yeasty dough, Yankee cooks quickly found a way of doing it better by devising a cutter which left a hole in the center.

Folklore says the original had a walnut in the center but some tightwad Yankee sea captain whose wife prepared barrels of the sinkers for his crew before each voyage, designed a cutter with a hole in the middle to eliminate the expensive nuts. This makes about as much sense as most of these hand-me-down legends perpetrated on the gullible, but it reads good.

Dutch Oven Sinkers

Add ½ cup of sugar to 2 cups of the expedition baking mix, with some grated nutmeg, 1 fresh egg or equivalent powdered, and enough canned cow or fresh milk to make a stiff dough. Break off into small chunks and fry in deep fat. This is an ideal way to season a new cast iron camp Dutch oven, incidentally.

Note: At high altitudes, have the fat less hot. Try about 350° at 6,000 feet.

IV

COOKING THE SOURDOUGH WAY

FOR THE MOST colorful character I ever knew in Alaska, back in the Dirty Thirties as a kid just out of high school, old Harvey took the cake—in this case the sourdough cake.

He was one of the first persons I met when I got off the northbound ship the last of October—when most people were going the other way. I had about ten centavos left after testing my skill and luck in the steerage compartment, with members of the ship's crew, a five-dollar sleeping bag, and no place to unroll it. I forget how I met Harvey, but remember he had just moved into town for the winter from his claim on Atlin Lake.

His "town house" was a one-room wannigan just outside Juneau on the road to the glacier. He let me spread my bag on the floor for a couple of weeks until I got settled, and also stuffed me daily with all manner of goodies made from a vile-looking crock of sourdough he kept behind the stove.

He made almost everything he cooked out of sourdough. And each time he made a pilgrimage to that fragrant pot—which had a scum of green slime around the edges, a layer of grain alcohol floating on top, and looked as deadly as carbolic acid—he would lovingly replace what he "borrowed" with fresh flour and water, and even the leavin's of the last meal.

He scoffed at any suggestion that his sourdough

starter might be a mite unsanitary or unhealthy. He said he'd been born and brought up on sourdough and expected to go on using it until the northern lights went out. He was about seventy-five or eighty then, and the last I heard he had lived to be ninety-one when booze finally got him.

After that introduction to the stuff, naturally the making of sourdough is a ritual around our house during the cold winter months, but while we've modernized the old Alaskan method of keeping a pot working behind the stove, there still is nothing that beats the smell of sourdough bread baking in the oven, or fluffy,

tangy sourdough hot cakes covered with melting butter and maple syrup on a lazy Saturday morning.

Anyone can make a sourdough starter. Just mix $2\frac{1}{2}$ cups of flour with enough lukewarm water to make a thick batter in a crock or plastic mixing bowl. Cover and set in a warm place to ferment. To speed things up, mix a tablespoon of dry active yeast with the batter, or use water from a pan of boiling potatoes.

The next day you should have a basic starter. To make batter from this, mix a cup or two of the starter with flour and warm water the night before you plan to use it. When this is ready, replenish the starter and use the rest for cooking.

For hot cakes that drive you wild with delight, mix a half cup of sourdough with one egg, half a cup of milk, half a cup of regular pancake mix (optional), one tablespoon of cooking oil, and a sprinkle of salt. Spoon the size hot cakes you like on a griddle already heated to about 380 degrees and lightly greased. For extra light and fluffy hot cakes, you can also use a quarter teaspoon of baking soda or baking powder.

For something a little more refined that you can (literally) sink your teeth into, try French bread. Dissolve a package of dry yeast in $1\frac{1}{2}$ cups of hot water, mix with one cup of sourdough starter in a large bowl, adding 4 cups of flour, 2 teaspoons of sugar, 2 teaspoons of salt. Cover with a piece of cloth and let it rise in a warm place until about twice its original size.

Then mix a cup of flour and a half teaspoon of baking soda or powder and stir into a stiff dough. Knead the dough on a board dusted with flour adding one more cup of flour—or just enough to make the dough smooth and shiny—and continue to knead.

Shape the dough into the size loaves desired, set on a

piece of greased paper or a sheet, cover and leave in a warm place until it has again doubled in size. Brush the top lightly with water, make a sharp slash in it and put in a 400-degree oven in a shallow pan with a little hot water in the bottom. Bake until an almond brown.

Sourdough also makes delicious biscuits, quick breads, breadsticks, blueberry muffins, waffles, bannock, or most anything in pastries.

The starter should be used and replenished at least every two weeks, or you may have to start it over. In between use keep it in a covered bowl in the refrigerator. It can also be frozen and kept indefinitely, and powdered starter is now available in packets for camping and hiking trips which needs no refrigeration.

There has been a lot of colorful hokum circulated about sourdough starters that have been kept going for nigh onto fifty years; or like the starter which the girls reputedly began in Dawson during the Klondike Rush and which is supposed to have spawned little starters all over the North Country.

Don't you believe it. A starter is easy to "lose," and often gets so worked out you want to replace it anyway. And why perpetuate a slimy-looking mess when it's so easy to make a new starter?

And besides, if you don't take care of yourself, it will get you in the end. Look what happened to old Harvey.

The first time I saw a batch of sourdough starter, however, was when my dad took me to the funeral of my grandfather at the old pioneer homestead in northern Wisconsin. I was about nine at the time.

Behind the stove in the kitchen lean-to was a one-gallon crock that had come over with my forebears from Sweden, and in it was a yeasty mixture that filled the kitchen with fumes like a brewery, and around the rim of the crock the slime and scum had gathered like moss on old hemlock.

When I wrinkled up my nose, my dad told me this was a sourdough starter and had been "cooking" since he was a little boy, always replenished after every use with leftover batter and scraps.

To me it looked something like a garbage disposal and I marveled that anyone could eat it and survive.

But Grandad lived on it all his life and survived until he was eighty-nine.

Most people today think of sourdough as a word for a grizzled tobacco-stained character plodding behind a burro in the Mojave or mushing behind a dog team up along the Yukon. The truth is "sourdough" is simply the term used to describe homemade yeast—a form of fermented dough used as a leaven in breadmaking, which has been a part of the art of cooking for at least six thousand years, and next to the honeybee, is one of man's most important discoveries.

Sourdough was the original yeast used until modern times when food chemistry discovered cheap and practical ways of making yeast available in cakes.

During the adventurous eras of the nineteenth and twentieth centuries when the mining and cattle frontiers inspired so much romantic literature, when the wilderness areas of Alaska, the Yukon, and the backwaters of the Old West were overrun with roving gents with a yen for gold or real-estate empires, sourdough out of sheer necessity became a staple of survival.

The term gradually was applied to those solitary veterans of the mountain and desert trails who never gave up looking for a pot of gold over the ridge, but took their sourdough pots along with them just in case.

In the wilderness a sourdough starter was the most important item in a man's outfit, something to be guarded at the expense of anything else, and many a tale has been told of this. The starter was the basis of practically every meal. From it one could manufacture not only bread, biscuits, and flapjacks, but feed the dogs, apply to burns and wounds, chink the log cabin, brew hootch, and, some say, even resole boots.

No camp cooking would be complete without sourdough. It fed generations of frontiersmen, miners, trappers, mountain men, and pioneers, and in spite of modern yeast, old-fashioned sourdough is still much used today. A working starter will keep for years if properly used, and there is almost no limit to the ways in which it may be employed in cooking, matters we will now take up in more detail.

The starter or "sponge" should be kept under refrigeration unless used every day; and even then should be used at least once a week. It can be kept frozen for long periods.

Later, when I was a lad growing up in North Dakota, my mother also kept a batch going during the winter months in a special place behind the old wood range. If she "lost" a batch, she simply brewed a new one. This is easy to do, and today it is even possible to purchase starters in powdered form which can be stored indefinitely until ready to mix and use, or to take along on a pack trip.

Here are some ways you can make your own starter.

Sourdough Starters

Starter No. 1. Mix 4 cups flour, 2 teaspoons salt, 2 teaspoons of sugar, and 4 cups of lukewarm potato water (water in which potatoes have been boiled) in a crock or jar and let stand in a warm place, loosely covered, for 3 or 4 days, or until fermentation begins. The process can be hurried by dissolving a yeast cake in a fourth cup of potato water.

Starter No. 2. Mix 2 cups flour, 2 cups lukewarm water, and 1 yeast cake or package of dry yeast. Let stand overnight in a warm place. By morning it should be bubbly with a pleasant yeasty smell.

Starter No. 3. Mix ¼ cup milk, ½ cup water, 2 teaspoons vegetable oil, and bring to a boil. Cool to lukewarm and dissolve 1 package of active dry yeast in ¼ cup warm water. Add 2 teaspoons sugar, 1½ teaspoons salt, and 2⅓ cups sifted flour, stirring liquid into flour just enough to blend thoroughly. Cover and let stand in a warm place for a half day or more. This makes enough starter for twelve loaves of bread.

Starter No. 4. Mix 1 cup plain flour and 1 cup lukewarm water in a scalded pot or jar, cover loosely, and let stand in a warm place to sour. This is the most primitive method and the result is often one of uncertainty regarding texture, odor, and flavor. If it doesn't work try one of the other methods. The use of modern yeast almost always assures a good starter on the first try.

A sourdough or sponge is your own private yeast factory. For best results keep it in a glass or pottery container, never in metal. The container should be well scalded to inhibit the growth of unwanted bacteria. When not in use, keep the starter in a cool place. It can be stored for long periods by freezing. On the trail in the old days the sourdough sponge was packed right in the flour bag. In cold weather starters lose some of their potency, but can be revived with a tablespoon of pure cider vinegar.

All sourdough cooking begins with the starter. From this the basic batter is mixed and enough withheld to replenish the starter in the pot. This batter is usually made by mixing a cup of starter with two cups or more of flour and two cups of lukewarm water. This is allowed to stand overnight in a warm place, or until it is fermenting. Then the pot is replenished and the balance of the batter used for mixing your sourdough bread, hot cakes, biscuits, or whatever.

Two secrets of good sourdough cookery are: *First*, avoid mixing the batter too much. Overmixing knocks the gases out of the dough that are needed for the raising process. It's best just to throw it together and let it go at that. *Second*, sourdough cookery requires slightly more heat than ordinary baking processes.

Never put anything back into the starter pot except the basic batter which has started to ferment. Especially do not put back any batter which has been mixed with sugar, salt, eggs, soda, or cooking oil.

Here's how to make sourdough bread using Starter No. 3:

To complete the recipe, bring ingredients to room temperature. Then add ½ cup milk, 1 cup water 1½ tablespoons vegetable oil, 1 package active dry yeast, 1½ tablespoons sugar, 2½ teaspoons salt, 4¾ cups flour, 2 tablespoons starter dough, ¼ cup warm water. Do this by combining milk, water, and oil, bringing to a boil, then cooling to lukewarm. Dissolve yeast in warm water, adding sugar and salt to cooled milk mixture. Put flour in a large bowl, hollow out center, and pour milk mixture into hole. Add starter and stir until blended, but do not knead.

Put dough in a greased bowl, cover and let rise until double. Divide into two even loaves and roll each into shape desired. Place on baking sheet and let rise uncovered in a lukewarm place until double. Bake 15 minutes at 425°, then 15 to 20 minutes longer at 350°. Brush with an egg white mixed with 1 tablespoon of cold water. Bake another 5 minutes. Cool in a drafty place.

By adding flour, milk, and eggs to about 2 tablespoons of this starter you can also make flapjacks.

Here are some other ways of making authentic sourdough flapjacks:

Sourdough Flapjacks

No. 1. Mix ½ cup of active starter, ½ cup pancake mix, 1 egg, 1 tablespoon cooking oil, ½ cup milk, ½ teaspoon soda. Lightly grease a hot griddle. Drop on griddle with large spoon while batter is still rising.

No. 2. Mix 1 cup starter, 1 cup flour, 1 egg, 2 tablespoons cooking oil, ¼ cup instant or evaporated milk. Blend in 1 teaspoon salt, 1 teaspoon soda, 2 tablespoons sugar. Let mixture bubble and foam a minute, then drop on hot griddle.

No. 3. Mix 2 cups starter, 2 cups flour, and 1 teaspoon baking soda, 2 well-beaten eggs or 1 tablespoon powdered eggs, 1 tablespoon sugar, 1 teaspoon salt. Stir in 2 or 3 tablespoons bacon fat, butter or suet, and cook on hot griddle.

Sourdough Biscuits

Mix 2 cups starter with ½ cup of flour to which has been blended 1 teaspoon of baking soda, 1 teaspoon salt, and 1 tablespoon of melted butter, bacon fat, or cooking oil. Add more flour if too thin, making a stiff dough. Lightly knead to form biscuits and drop in buttered pans. Allow to rise double, brush with melted butter, and bake at about 400° in Dutch oven for a few minutes, then reduce heat and cook until done, about 45 minutes. You can also make bread this way, forming loaves instead of biscuits.

Sourdough Donuts

Mix ½ cup sourdough batter, 2 egg yolks, or 1 whole egg, ½ cup sugar, 1 tablespoon shortening, ⅓ cup sour milk or buttermilk, 2 cups flour, 1 teaspoon baking powder, ½ teaspoon soda, ½ teaspoon salt, ¼ teaspoon nutmeg, ¼ teaspoon cinnamon. First sift dry ingredients together, and stir into liquid. If possible chill or let dough stand before rolling out and cutting. Deep fry in Dutch oven.

V

FIXIN' THE WILD ONES

IN MAY, 1804, when the Lewis and Clark expedition left Wood River and leaped off into the unknown West, not to return for two years, four months, and ten days, the men embarked on an adventure comparable in those times to the first astronaut flight to the moon today.

Not only was their journey filled with unknown dangers, but it was an undertaking for which the simple logistics of supply were overwhelming.

How did history's most famous overland journey manage to cross, on foot and by canoe, more than eight thousand miles of raw Indian territory without maps and credit cards, without electronic communications, without refrigeration, and even without the aid of the friendly nearby motor club tow truck?

The permanent party, from Fort Mandan on, was made up of wilderness-tested, young, tough, adventurous, self-sufficient young men in their late teens and early twenties. Their commanders were not only amazingly compatible and experienced, in spite of their youth, but certainly can be described as two of the most talented and able leaders this nation has ever produced.

Moreover, the expedition—in spite of the folklore and romanticism that latter-day women novelists have confused history with—was perhaps the best armed, best fed, and best equipped hunting and fishing excursion ever undertaken—and at government expense, too.

For example, besides some twelve thousand pounds of food brought along, such as salt, pepper, flour, parched meal, shelled corn, coffee, sugar, tea, lard, whiskey, brandy, rum, and "portable soup," the corps' hunters killed, according to my painstaking search of their daily journals, in round numbers about 3,000 deer, 800 elk, 600 buffalo, 400 antelope (pronghorn), tons of waterfowl of all kinds, plus tremendous quantities of fish, bear (for oil), cougar, moose, and bighorn sheep—the latter being the greatest delicacy that any frontier ever offered.

The party also consumed with more or less relish: wild berries and fruits, greens, Indian corn, squash, watermelon, pumpkin, herbs and roots, as well as frequent side dishes of coyote, wolf, crow, fox, badger, eagle, gopher, hawk, squirrel, wildcat, raccoon, otter, muskrat, beaver, shrimp, mussels, turtle, dogmeat, horsemeat, seal meat, whale blubber, and even mushrooms—a food then almost unknown in the American diet, and, fortunately for history, in this instance only the nontoxic varieties were sampled.

The least popular of all this overwhelming bill of fare—as might be expected of GI's even then—was the 193 pounds of portable soup prepared for the expedition by Francois Baillet in his shop at 21 North Ninth in Philadelphia. Sort of a colonial K-ration, it did help save the party from starvation on the only critical leg of the journey, across the Bitterroot Mountains.

The party had a large supply of fishing gear including hooks, gigs, a sportsman's "flaske," and eight "stave reels," obtained by Lewis from the Old Experienced Tackle Shop at No. 32 Great Dock Street in Philadelphia.

From one to ten men, in addition to George Drouillard and later John Colter and the Fields brothers, daily were assigned to provide fresh meat. Hunting was considered the best duty and even the commanders often tramped along shore ahead of the boats on shooting excursions.

The first buffalo was killed by Joseph Fields above the mouth of the Kansas River. The humps, marrowbones, and tongues of these animals were prized most —but frontiersmen who came later were unanimous in their opinion that buffalo surpassed any other kind of game (except the rare wild sheep), including domestic beef.

At "Cat Fish Camp," August 14, 1804, a fishing party took 800 fish with a homemade seine, including 79 pike, 8 "salmon," 1 rock, 1 flatback, 127 buffalo fish and redhorse, 4 bass, 490 catfish, and many small silver fish and freshwater shrimp.

Indians along the way introduced them to bois roule or kinnikinnic, a native tobacco, and to Indian bread-fruit (*Psorealea esculenta*) a turnip-like root which could be eaten raw or cooked.

Their diet also included native foods such as lamb's-quarter, watercress, and the wild peanut (*Amphicarpa monica*) robbed from the nests of field mice.

At the Big Bend of the Missouri, 1,600 miles from St. Louis in what is now North Dakota, they camped for the winter of 1804-5 with the Mandans. Here they found the Indians cultivating corn, pumpkins, beans, and other garden stuffs unknown to most white men. Here during the cold, bleak winter the hunting parties killed thousands of pounds of game, much of it too lean and tough for good eating. They brought it in on sleighs pulled by dogs and horses and stacked the carcasses like cordwood outside the huts.

The men celebrated Christmas with extra rations of tafia, a crude frontier rum, as the temperatures dropped to forty below zero. A favorite Mandan dish was a mixture of pumpkin, beans, corn, and chokecherries boiled together.

Once beyond the mouth of the Little Missouri, the party—now including Toussaint Charbonneau and his seventeen-year-old Shoshone wife Sacajawea, and their two-month-old son, Little Pomp—entered a region unknown to civilized man. If game had been abundant on the plains, now the fecundity of wildlife was almost beyond comprehension. Wildfowl filled the skies and blackened the ponds and lakes. On the hills and in the coulees, buffalo, deer, elk, antelope, and their predators and camp followers appeared in unbroken herds in all directions as far as the men could see.

The men filled up on fresh meat, eggs, fowl, buffalo humps, beaver tails, bighorn loins, wild artichokes, onions, and even wild licorice.

In June, below the Great Falls, Lewis came down with dysentery. He cured himself with a brew of chokecherry twigs. Meanwhile Silas Goodrich, the expedition's irrepressible fisherman, went off looking for a good hole and caught a half-dozen trout from seventeen to twenty-three inches long. Some of the others killed three fat cow buffalo.

"My fare is really sumptuous this evening," Lewis wrote, "buffaloe's humps, tongues, and marrowbones, fine trout, parched meal, pepper and salt, and a good appetite—the last of which," he added, smacking his lips, "is not considered the least of the luxuries."

In the Bitterroot country the party tasted its first Pacific salmon. Once Goodrich and some men dragged a stream and netted 528 trout and "mullet" (probably whitefish).

On the descent of the Clearwater, Snake, and Columbia, the party lived on dried berries, fresh and pounded salmon, acorns, dogmeat, bear oil, and camas roots.

John Collins, one of the corps' most dedicated drinking men, who had not imbibed since the previous July 4, joyfully discovered how to make a kind of beer out of the "pa-shi-coquar-marsh" root.

On the lower Columbia they found ducks and geese, elk and bear, and another new species of deer, the Columbia blacktail. A staple of the Indians was wappato, or sagittafolia, the bulb of which was well known in China where it was cultivated.

On Christmas Day, 1805, at Fort Clatsop, Clark wrote: "... The day proved Showery wet and disagreeable ... our Diner concisted of pore Elk, so much Spoiled that we eate it thro' mear necessity, Some Spoiled pounded fish and a fiew roots."

The saltworks, established at what is now Seaside, produced about a gallon a day for the return trip. Clark heard about a whale washed up on the beach and with a party went over Tillamook Head and purchased three hundred pounds from the Indians. Some found it resembled the beaver in flavor, others said it tasted like the fat of pork.

The men ate sturgeon, candlefish or eulachon (smelt), seal meat, and other local dishes. Since thirty out of the thirty-three in the party smoked or chewed tobacco, they soon discovered a substitute in the bark of the red willow.

On the trip home, once they again reached the fruitful prairies of Montana and the Dakotas, the men rejoiced. The journals constantly referred to the fact that the party, when it lived off buffalo and similar game, was at its healthiest and strongest.

At the mouth of the Yellowstone, Lewis was accidentally shot in the rump by Pierre Cruzatte, the expedition's fiddler and canoe expert, who was blind in one eye and couldn't see well out of the other.

This was the West's first recorded hunting accident.

On August 14 they reached the Mandan villages again, and September 3 they met some traders from St. Louis with news of home, fresh tobacco, and whiskey. On September 20 they touched the little French outpost of La Charette, where the aged Daniel Boone now lived. On September 22, they landed at the army cantonment near Coldwater Creek—and on September

24, Clark recorded in his journals what must have been a granddaddy of a hangover, as he rose early to begin writing his reports—after all this was a military operation.

It was also the longest, writin'est, shootin'est, eatin'est, fishin'est cross-country adventure ever recorded in American tradition.

And one of their most valued pieces of equipment, toted all the way up the Missouri, across the Bitterroots, and down the Columbia to the Pacific, and back home again, was a large-sized Dutch oven.

The camp Dutch oven is the only sure device for cooking wild game satisfactorily under most conditions. Most attempts to fry, broil, and roast tough steaks or

old birds results in something that tastes like an old knapsack. Wild meat is not marbled like domestic beef. The basic Dutch-oven method, with its initial searing in hot fat and the long period of slow simmering under cover, can make even the toughest wild game so tender that the meat falls away from the bones. In this the Dutch oven can be likened to a low, slow pressure cooker. As a rule, don't use the fat of a wild animal (except bear).

Cariboo Stew

This is the way my old friend Harvey Smith made it up in the Cariboo country. Trappers depend upon stew—and all of them make it a different way, depending on what's available at the moment. Almost always, though, the North Country trapper used a heavy iron camp Dutch oven and cooked his stews slo-o-owly. The long, slow cooking released juices that blended with each other.

The trapper usually made his stew from elk, moose, caribou, or deer in the following ratio: 2 pounds of meat or wild game, half dozen carrots cut into chunks, 1 bay leaf, salt and pepper to taste, half-dozen potatoes, chunked, 1 small cabbage, cut, and a half-dozen small onions.

First cube the meat and brown in bacon fat in the bottom of the Dutch oven. Cover with water and simmer over low heat. In about an hour add carrots, salt and pepper, and bay leaf. Half an hour later add the potatoes and onions and enough water to cover the meat. Later add the cabbage and cook until tender. Season to taste and pitch in.

Thicken the pan juices with a little flour or cornstarch paste made with cold water, stirring in until thick as desired.

Roast Antelope

You'll need a shoulder or ham to fit your size Dutch oven. Rub roast with flour, salt and pepper, brown in fat or suet. Remove roast from oven and saute 3 or 4 slices of onion in the same fat. Put roast back and add 2 cans tomatoes, 1/2 cup diced celery, 3 cups dry red wine, 1 bay leaf, a sprig of parsley, and a pinch of marjoram, rosemary, thyme. Cook slowly until done. Then add a can of mushrooms to the gravy and serve with rice.

Baked Trout

Preheat Dutch oven and lid and grease the pot. Clean and slit fresh-caught trout and place in oven, belly up. Sprinkle with salt and pepper, cross with strips of bacon. Put lid on and set oven on hot coals. Cover lid with coals. In 15 or 20 minutes remove lid and pour a sauce over fish. You can make this out of melted butter and lemon juice.

Roast Venison

Soak a clean cloth in vinegar and wipe clean a chunk of venison. Roll in flour that has been salted and peppered. Drop a gob of suet into preheated Dutch oven. Sear meat on all sides. Lay strips of bacon across roast fastened with toothpicks. Hang rings of onions on toothpicks. Pour in 1/2 cup hot water, 1 can of tomato soup, spices and condiments as desired Cover and simmer for a couple of hours or until done. Make a delicious gravy out of the pan juices.

Don Buffalo's Frog Legs

When I was ten years old, my pal Jake and I went into the frog-leg business. It was unsuccessful because we couldn't keep from eating our inventory. We cooked them like this, fresh out of Downing's Creek:

Trim and clean the legs, skin them, sprinkle with salt and pepper, and roll them in beaten eggs and crumbs. Drop in deep frying fat for about 3 minutes. Drain and serve.

Grouse, Partridge, or Prairie Chicken

After cleaning birds, brown in preheated oven with hot suet. Add hot water to pot and about 1/4 cup of cream for each bird, poured over meat. Roast until done.

Oven-fried Squirrel

Wash and wipe the squirrels with a vinegar-soaked cloth. Cut into serving pieces. Prepare a mixture of 1 slightly beaten egg, 1 1/2 teaspoons pepper, 2 tablespoons water, 1 1/2 teaspoons salt. Dip pieces of meat into mixture and roll in fine bread crumbs. Brown in preheated oven with a chunk of melted suet. Cover and cook slowly until done.

Serve on boiled rice with brown gravy if you like. To make the gravy, drain off all fat in pan except 3 tablespoons. Blend in 3 tablespoons flour, 1 teaspoon salt, and 1/4 teaspoon pepper. Cook, stirring until brown, boiling a couple of minutes. Stir in 1 1/2 cups of hot water or pan juice.

Wild Rice

Wild rice (by which is usually meant the rice gathered and marketed by the Indians in northern Minnesota), is a traditional side dish for wild game. To prepare it, wash several times. Soak in warm water for four hours. Cook on a low fire for one-half hour. Do not stir. Drain and then:

Fry lightly in butter, or fry in bacon grease with a boiled chopped green pepper, or fry in butter with mushrooms.

Buffalo a la Dutch Oven

Good buffalo meat is the finest of all beef—and it's still available in limited quantities from private and government herds in the United States and Canada during the fall culling season, and from occasional controlled shoots.

This recipe is also good for any tough beef or game.

Melt about 3 tablespoons of suet or shortening in the bottom of preheated oven and sear a 6- or 7-pound chunk of meat. Blend 1½ tablespoons vinegar, 1 teaspoon nutmeg, 1 tablespoon ginger, 1 tablespoon cinnamon, 1 tablespoon of salt, and ¼ tablespoon of pepper with 1½ cups of water and 2½ cups of apple juice. Pour over meat. Sprinkle 1 cup of chopped onions on top and 1 teaspoon garlic. You can also add a small can of tomato sauce.

Set lid on and simmer slowly until done. Make a gravy from the pan juices. Then get out of the way or you'll get stomped on by a herd of hungry buffalo hunters.

Prairie Rabbit

Sear a rabbit in hot oven with bacon fat, suet, or shortening and season as desired. Add a small amount of hot water and set lid on. Replenish water as necessary until meat is steamed off bones, which should take about three to four hours.

Hasenpfeffer

Cut up rabbit and place pieces in a crock with a mixture of 1 cup vinegar and one cup water, to which has been added 1 sliced onion, 1 teaspoon salt, ½ teaspoon pepper, and ½ teaspoon whole cloves. Cover tightly and soak for forty-eight hours.

Remove meat and save juice. Dry and roll the meat in a mixture of flour, salt, and pepper and brown in shortening or suet. Slowly mix 1 cup of the juice into the pot. Simmer until meat is done. Before serving stir in 1 cup sour cream and heat but do not boil. Add small chunks of boiled potato if desired.

Roast Rabbit

In a preheated Dutch oven place 1 pound of pork and a couple of teaspoons of suet or lard. Cut up rabbit and add to pot. Sear meat on all sides. Salt and pepper to taste, add ½ cup water, some chopped onions, and simmer for a couple of hours, adding water if necessary. Add vegetables such as carrots, potatoes, and complete cooking.

Don's Buffalo and Beer Bust

4 lbs. buffalo meat	2 tbsp. tomato puree
3 medium onions	1 pint beer
3 carrots	herb bag of garlic clove,
3 potatoes	bay leaf, parsley, 3
3 tbsp. flour	cloves, thyme
2 pints beef stock	salt, pepper

Cut meat into small cubes, season, roll in flour, brown in oil in a heavy saucepan or Dutch oven. Cube onions and saute in the oil, adding to meat. Then add liquids and herb bag to the meat and vegetables and simmer until tender. Remove herb bag, dish out stew into plates or into individual pot pie oven dishes, cover with pastry, brush with milk, and bake until golden brown.

Prairie Bannock

3 cups flour	1 tsp. salt
2 tbsp. baking powder	1 tbsp. sugar
2 tbsp. lard	3 cups cold water

Mix and stir ingredients in cold water to make a batter, stirring rapidly and pouring quickly into a greased Dutch oven lid or bottom. Bake for 35 to 45 minutes at 400°.

Serve with melted butter and wild berry jelly or preserves, or honey. Bannock will keep for days without drying up or becoming moldy.

Dutch Oven Antelope

Pound several thick antelope steaks with flour, salt, dry mustard, pepper to taste, and brown in hot fat in the oven. Add milk, sliced onion, and chopped celery so steaks are just submerged, put lid on and simmer for an hour or so. The pot liquor can then be made into gravy by thickening with flour.

Pemmican

Grind up jerky in food grinder or pound into powder, mix sugar and raisins or dried berries to taste and then stir in melted suet and when cool store in plastic bags. Use an equal amount of lean meat and suet, and about an ounce or two of dried berries and 2 tablespoons of sugar for every pound of meat.

Deer Treat
In a preheated Dutch oven saute sliced onions for about 5 minutes and then season with salt, pepper, paprika. In a moment add deer heart or tongue or both to the mixture, after cutting into bite-size chunks.

Deer Stew
You can use the neck and other lean miscellaneous parts for this one, cutting into small pieces and dredging in a bag of flour. Brown in the hot Dutch oven in melted suet and remove, then saute a sliced onion with a minced clove of garlic for three minutes, and return the meat to the pot with enough boiling water to form a thick stew. Season with salt, pepper, thyme, parsley, and diced celery Simmer for one to two hours depending on the amount of meat, then add cut potatoes and several small onions and cook a half hour longer. Make a gravy from the pot juices.

Braised Duck
Melt a large chunk of butter in a preheated Dutch oven and brown two medium-sized ducks. Add a quart of boiling water and enough salt, pepper, thyme, garlic, and cloves to season. Add chopped onions and diced carrots. Cover and simmer for one to two hours. Make a thick gravy from the juices.

Seared Elk
With hot bacon drippings in a preheated Dutch oven, sear a couple pounds of elk roast and cover with a barbecue sauce. Cook for one to two hours in a moderate heat. To make a sauce use 1 cup of tomato catsup, ¼ cup vinegar, 2 tbsps. Worcestershire, 1 patty of butter,

2 slices lemon or 1 tbsp. of lime juice, 1 chopped onion, 1 tbsp. salt, ¼ tsp. cinnamon and allspice.

Idaho Moose Shank

Put a large chunk of moose shank in a Dutch oven with water, salt, pepper, garlic salt, thyme, marjoram, and bay leaf. When brought to a boil, simmer until meat is tender. Then add potato chunks, celery stalk, small onions and carrots. Bring to a boil again and simmer until vegetables are done.

Soused Moose

Saute 3 small onions and 2 cloves of garlic in a Dutch oven in a half cup of olive oil. Rub a suitable rump roast of moose with crushed rosemary, season and brown. Cover and simmer for a couple hours or so, then add small amount of red wine, 2 cans mushrooms, cup of chopped ripe olives, and a can of tomato juice. Simmer some more until ready to eat.

Columbia River Smelt Chowder

Smelt dippers drool over the first mess of fried smelt when the run appears about February in the lower Columbia tributaries. The second mess they can't even give away. These rich little eulachon or candlefish are delicious but surfeiting. But here's a way to enjoy them the rest of the year, too.

Use them instead of other fish in your favorite chowder. All you have to remember is that the flavor of smelt is richer and more delicate, and that it requires an experimentation with ingredients. The Manhattan type chowder works best with smelt, using tomato juice instead of milk.

Fry out ½ lb. of salt pork in Dutch oven. Remove pork and in the fat fry a medium chopped onion. Add 2 cans of tomatoes with juice, 2 cups boiling water, 1 lb. of smelt, 1 lb. of chopped potatoes, a bay leaf, chopped celery, salt and pepper to taste, 1 tbsp. horseradish. Cook for half hour or until potatoes are done and stir in the pork.

Dutch Oven Turtle

Cut turtle meat into chunks, using all the edible parts including the heart. Soak briefly in lemon or lime juice, reconstituted if you don't have fresh. Dip in beaten egg, roll in flour and cornmeal, and season with salt, pepper, paprika, and other condiments to taste. Brown in hot fat in the preheated Dutch oven. Reduce heat and add 2 or 3 cups water, sliced onion and chopped celery, and simmer until ready.

Woodchuck Pot Roast

Dredge chunks of young woodchuck in flour which has been seasoned with your favorite condiments and brown in hot fat in a preheated Dutch oven. Then add a cup of boiling water, 3 tbsps. of lime juice, and simmer for three or four hours. Before serving add ½ cup wine if desired.

VI

SMOKING, JERKING, AND OTHER DELIGHTFUL ARTS

Smoking and Kippering

There have been many theories advanced on how the West was won, but the truth is it was really won on the stomach—just like Napoleon, or somebody, said it would be.

In frontier days, before modern technology of food preservation and artificial refrigeration, folks got along—and indeed produced some mighty tough hombres—because they practiced the arts of sourdough cookery, drying and smoking meat and jerky, and making such staples as pemmican.

Many of these arts, which were once necessary to survival, have been revived simply because technology has not been able to reproduce the essential qualities of taste and nutrition found in Old West foods.

For example, the unique taste and goodness of properly smoked or kippered meat, fish, and fowl cannot be duplicated in any other way except by these traditional, centuries-old processes.

Most folks seem to think that smoking and kippering is a complicated process requiring a huge outdoor structure and a couple of attendants to keep the fires going around the clock for days on end.

Not so. Smoking and kippering is the simplest food processing known to man. It takes only a few minutes of your time over a period of a few hours at most. It isn't necessary to build an open fire or go through any fancy folklore or hocus-pocus.

You can build a small smoker for use on your patio for a few dollars from plans obtained from Oregon State University Extension Service. Or you can buy a small, aluminum, portable model from any sporting goods or hardware store, operated by a simple heating element.

We chose a small commercial unit that retails for just over $30 and comes with chips enough to last all summer. We figured the cost of buying plywood and building our own—even in a region where plywood is produced—would have at least equaled this, and the unit would not have been so convenient and portable.

We sent for various government bulletins on smoking and kippering and, upon studying these, came to the conclusion that there are no complicated rules or procedures—each person will find by personal experimentation the best methods for his purpose.

The smoking or kippering process can be broken down into three simple steps:

1. Soaking the meat, fish, or fowl in a seasoned salt brine, or in some cases blanching or marinating instead of soaking.

2. Curing it in the smoker for the prescribed length of time.

3. Finishing it off in the oven, in some instances.

We discovered that you don't have to smoke it continuously. You can stop, if necessary, and start in again later or the next day.

We discovered also that most recipes call for too much brining or seasoning for our own taste, and that most of the smoking times given in the manuals and bulletins are too long.

We prefer blanching and marinating the meat before smoking, in preference to the soaking in brine, but this is a matter of personal taste: All fish should be brined, of course.

Fowl is best when lightly smoked and then finished off in the oven. The smoker should be preheated before putting in meat and fish. Many cuts of meat can be given a delicious taste by smoking for an hour before cooking. The meat or fish must be thoroughly dry before putting it in the smoker, otherwise it will steam. Also the smoking process must be done at very low heat to prevent cooking—smoking is essentially a drying process, not a cooking one.

Speaking of drying meat, the most successful and delicious of all is smoked jerky. We first marinated (and also tried blanching with equal success) the strips of beef, then gave them an hour's smoking, and finally completed the drying out in the oven. Superb is the word. Set oven at the lowest temperature and leave the door ajar.

Contrary to what the books said, the best results are obtained with the best cuts of meat and fish, and then after removing as much bone and waste as possible.

Another trick learned was to remove quickly the cover and let in some fresh air if the smoker seemed slow to start again after putting fresh chips on the hot plate.

One more thing: The only difference between smoking and kippering is that the former is "cold smoking" at low temperatures, and the latter is "hot smoking" at higher temperatures.

The two basic methods impart different flavor, and in general the kippered product does not keep long, whereas smoked fish and meat keep indefinitely (but not around our house—it disappears quickly).

Smoking and kippering are two arts which have not died out, and don't deserve to, for there is scarcely a tastier way of preparing and preserving foods in one simple operation.

Helpful Hints

Use only fresh meat, fish, and game for smoking.

Do not use aluminum containers for brining.

To keep fish and meat from sticking to racks, rub racks with vegetable oil or shortening.

Always remove heads, tails, bones, and waste from fish and game first.

Do not allow the fish or meat to "cook."

Keep smoked foods under refrigeration. If a surface mold develops, cut it off or wipe clean with vinegar.

Do not over-brine or over-smoke the meat or fish.

Do not allow smudge to burst into open flame.

Fish and meat must be dry, with all loose moisture removed.

Do not permit any moisture inside the smoker.

Do not use a resinous wood such as pine or fir.

Preparing fish such as bass, carp, or pickerel, dip fish in hot water and skin before brining.

Sometimes chilling brine with ice improves fish preparation.

Hot Smoking, Kippering

Immerse in brine for twelve to twenty-four hours. Remove to fresh water. Freshen for two to four hours. Drain well and dry with cloth or paper. Oil trays to prevent sticking, place meat on trays, and put in smoker. Process with warm smoke (around 100 degrees) for four to six hours for flavor, then at oven heat (up to 150 degrees) to thoroughly cook.

Cool Smoking

Brine for specified time but do not wash in fresh water. For a sweeter product add brown sugar to brine. Drain and dry thoroughly and place in smoker at temperatures not exceeding 90 degrees for one to five days until done. Smoking need not be a continuous process, but best to finish as rapidly as possible. Meat may be cooked before eating if desired. If jerky is wanted, leave meat in smoker without heat longer, or remove to warming oven for further drying.

Flavoring

Tobasco, onions, garlic, cloves, cider, vinegar, brown sugar, bay leaves, seafood and poultry seasonings, and other condiments may be added to the brining water in addition to salt, depending on taste.

Types of Smokers

wood barrels	plywood
steel drums	scrap lumber
cardboard boxes	"log cabin"
old icebox	sheetmetal
old refrigerator	washtub

(using electric hot plate or open combustion)

Blanching: Dip meat not more than one minute in boiling water containing seasonings. Dry thoroughly and sprinkle with seasoning. Put in smoker.

Marinating: Soak in a seasoning mixture with tenderizer and Italian dressing for two hours. Dry and put in smoker.

Products Which Can Be Smoke Cured

Seafood	Game	Domestic
salmon	deer	pork chops
trout	elk	spareribs
sturgeon	bear	roasts
smelt	waterfowl	steaks
catfish	upland birds	tongue
whitefish	muskrat	loins
shad	beaver	hams
herring	moose	cheeses
steelhead	woodchucks	liver
oysters	duck	kidneys
clams	goose	heart
suckers	pheasant	jerky
carp	rabbits	sausage
squawfish	jerky	wieners
kokanee	giblets	brains

Woods To Use

alder	hickory
maple	ash
cherry	dry corncobs
apple	vine maple
beech	any hardwood
	(remove bark)

How To Make Jerky

Ever wonder how Lewis and Clark managed to pack along enough fresh meat to feed a crew of thirty-three hungry young adventurers? I thought not.

When you stop to think that they had no means of refrigeration, and could only keep what they could pack, it turns out to be a major problem, yet the expedition ate sumptuously whenever red meat was available.

The secret is, they "jerked" all the meat they did not immediately consume.

Jerky is simply dried raw meat. Repeat: uncooked dehydrated meat. It takes about five pounds of raw meat to make one pound of jerky, which makes it one of the most concentrated edibles known to man. It's also one of the easiest to prepare.

Because it's called "jerky," this doesn't mean you cut hunks of raw meat and start jerking at it. The process, of course, has been known for centuries and is one of the reasons the Spaniards—probably the greatest explorers and adventurers ever to hit the North and South American continents—were able to cross long distances on foot.

The word "jerky," naturally, comes from *charqui*, which means "dried beef."

Jerky in recent years has made a big comeback in popularity among outdoorsmen, especially those who have taken to backpacking and in their constant search for lighter gear and more concentrated foods, have discovered they can prepare the best right in their own homes at a fraction of the cost of commercial dehydrated foods.

Moreover they've discovered that jerky makes a highly delicious snack food, appetizer, and smorgasbord. On the trail, three or four ounces and a canteen of water will keep a hiker going all day. It takes only a couple of light strips to make an entire meal. Jerky has a high nutritional value, lacking only vitamin C, and animal fats. It has a long life, will keep for weeks and months without refrigeration in the field, and indefinitely in cool storage.

And, even if it is raw dried flesh, and looks like a piece of old shoe that's been lying in the street too long, it only takes one bite and a flow of juices over your tastebuds to change all your inhibitions. Once you've tasted the spicy, juicy tang of jerky, you'll become a convert.

Lewis and Clark and other frontiersmen considered jerking meat just another necessary chore and seldom wasted much imagination on it. They simply strapped out long strips of flesh and laid them upon rocks, or hung them on bushes in the sun to dehydrate. Frequently they assisted the process by building a smudge under the meat, which also helped keep the flies off. During the winter rains at Fort Clatsop they hung their elk meat in the meat room next to the orderly room and kept a smoky fire going all the time under the meat.

You have a choice of two ways—the bush method and the home kitchen method.

The flesh of any lean red-meated game animal such as deer, moose, elk, buffalo, or caribou, or domestic beef, can be used. In the field method, cut in strips one-half inch thick and hang in the sun, or in any dry place where the water content can evaporate. Game meat should perhaps be soaked in saltwater first for about five minutes. In coastal areas sea water can be used for this.

If you have salt and pepper available, the meat can be seasoned before drying.

Outdoors a smoky fire should be built under the meat, since it takes several days for the sun and wind to do the job. At night or when it rains, the meat should be protected.

In the home method, obtain some cuts of beef at the

market—round steak yields less waste and is easiest to prepare. Carefully remove all fat and muscle, then season with salt, pepper, oregano, marjoram, basil, thyme, smoky condiments, or what have you, pounding the seasoning into the meat.

Cut the meat into strips about one-half inch thick along the grain—not across the grain like a roast.

Spread out on the wire cake racks used in your oven and turn the heat up to about 120°. Leave the door partly open so the moisture can escape. Heat about four hours and then turn over and heat the other side for about the same time, or until the meat has shriveled up, turned black, and there is no moisture in the center.

When done the strips should be dry clean through but flexible enough to bend without snapping. The important thing is not to hurry the process. Venison will turn out blacker and more brittle than domestic beef, but all of it will become more brittle as the pieces cool off.

Put foil under the racks to catch the drippings during the process. Any fat left in the meat will quickly turn rancid. Use much more seasoning than you think is necessary because the drying process weakens their effect. Try a small batch on your first attempt. Don't pound the meat so much that you break down the fibres. Do not "cook" the meat.

Smoked jerky can also be made in an outdoors smoker, but using hickory chips in a pan on a hot plate during the early part of the process.

When ready to use, simply bite off a small chunk, let it work around in your mouth to start the juices flowing, and then, as you begin to savor the tang, look out—you're hooked on the stuff.

It can be used as is for trail food, noontime snacks

during hikes and hunts, and as appetizers. For an all-around food in the field, try making pemmican with it, as explained elsewhere in this book.

Tips On Cooking Game

For fried rabbit, soak the skinned and cleaned animals overnight in water to which a tablespoon of soda has been mixed. Cut into small chunks and parboil until tender. Then dry and roll in flour, and pop in hot skillet with 2 tablespoons of suet or lard. Cover and cook slowly with onions and seasoning.

To clean ducks and geese, clip the tips of the wings off and pull out coarse outer feathers, leaving the bird covered with fuzzy down. Melt a package of paraffin in a pail of hot water and dunk birds. Remove and drop in cold water until wax has hardened. Peel off the coating of wax and the feathers will come with it. Clean thoroughly and draw.

For roasting soak in salt water for a couple of hours, or in a mixture of vinegar and water. Do not parboil as this will make the meat dry and spoil the flavor.

Pheasants and similar upland birds are best skinned and cut into serving pieces before cooking.

When roasting wild duck without dressing, place an onion or carrot in the cavity, and perhaps a whole unpeeled apple. Lay strips of bacon or salt pork across the breast of the bird. Baste frequently.

Big game roasts are prepared the same way as beef. Sear or brown first and then cook slowly. Venison needs more moisture than beef. Use onions generously. Mushrooms fried in butter are also good with venison.

The trimmings from ribs and other cuts of deer and elk can be used for hamburger or meatballs or meat loaf. Grind as with round steak, but mix about one part pork steak or sausage to three parts of wild game.

Pemmican the Authentic Way

Pound and shred an amount of jerky equal to the same amount of raw animal fat (preferably domestic animal) or suet which has been cut into small chunks.

First try out the fat in a pan over a slow fire, being careful it does not boil. When ready, pour the hot melted fat over the shredded jerky and mix together thoroughly and quickly. Do not use any salt or condiments. If a flavor is desired mix in raisins, dried blueberries, serviceberries, or even dried chopped peaches or apricots.

Pack the pemmican in commercial sausage casings or in suitable plastic bags.

Pemmican is a trail food that has never been equaled by modern science. It contains every necessary mineral, vitamin, or food element to sustain active physical life except vitamin C. Since a healthy man can last about fifty or sixty days without this—and in the northern hemisphere, it is readily available in such plants as rose hips—there is no real problem. Several rose hips will supply all the necessary vitamin C for the hardest day, and prevent scurvy.

Pemmican will keep for weeks and months without refrigeration, and indefinitely in a cool, dry place.

It should be stressed that although jerky is a wonderfully nourishing trail food, it is not good alone for long periods of strenuous activity for it lacks fats and certain food elements.

Butchering and Caring for Game

It's probably safe to say that 75 percent of all venison brought home by hunters these days is ruined or wasted to one degree or another. This is because few citified people these days know how to care for wild game, how to age it, keep it, and prepare it for the table. Because of this a lot of good eating winds up in the garbage can, and a lot of noses get turned up at the very suggestion of a wild game dinner.

Since most butcher shops either refuse or dislike to handle big game animals, it behooves the mighty hunter to learn how to take care of his own. Techniques of boning up deer for amateurs have been worked out by the Oregon State University Extension Service and others, by which you can fully utilize and enjoy your game.

The deer boning method developed at Oregon State University was adapted from the ancient one used by Northwest Indians for centuries—and still used on the reservations. It's easy to learn, can be done in the home, and the meat requires much less space in the freezer or locker. Complete details can be obtained from bulletins and other literature usually available free from these agencies.

However, since the first step in boning deer is to study the suggested boning chart of major cuts, the chart used for one method is reproduced on page 86.

Most hunters forget, too, that ground venison mixed with other meat makes delicious meatballs, mooseburgers, wieners, and salami and bologna, to say nothing of excellent jerky and pemmican.

In spite of the rapid urbanization of America in the Space Age, wild game continues to be an important culinary adventure—not as important, of course, as it was in frontier times when much of a family's diet

Venison Boning Chart
(Location of Main Cuts)

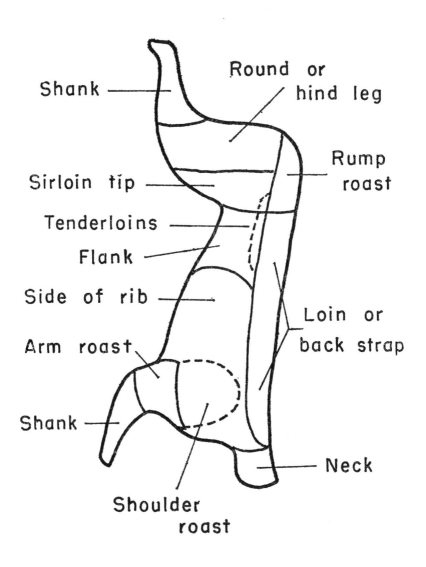

depended upon the hunt, but much more important than many folks realize.

The diaries and journals of early fur traders and explorers, men like John C. Fremont, make frequent mention of scarcity of game as they passed through certain sections such as the Oregon Country. Today state and federal wildlife biologists have managed to bring back many species and maintain them at levels consistent with the range and habitat. Today more than twenty-five million Americans enjoy the hunt, and most of them bring home game.

For example, around the turn of the century, an Oregon game director, in his annual report, stated that never again would elk be hunted in that state. Today, as many as 12,000 elk are killed by hunters each year in a regular open season. In the same state an average of 120,000 deer are shot each season for a total of more than 12,000 tons of venison for the festive tables.

The wild turkey, a true native of North America, once found in thirty-eight states—mainly in the East, South, and Middle States, today survives and prospers in about twenty states from Pennsylvania to Florida, westward to Arizona, and south into Mexico. In addition, the wild turkey—a wary, sly, alert bird weighing up to twenty pounds—is being successfully introduced into states such as Oregon and Idaho where it had never been before. About 500,000 of these birds are killed in annual hunts.

The lowly rabbit has for generations furnished sport for millions of youngsters growing up in rural areas. About fifty million are killed by hunters each year (figuring "rabbit" to mean both hare and rabbit, such as the cottontail, jack, pigmy, marsh, brush, snowshoe, and other varieties).

Young, tender rabbits have light meat and can be cooked like young, tender chicken. Larger rabbits, with dark flesh, should be braised, stewed, or marinated in the same way as chicken.

It's interesting to note that the rabbit (or hare) is nature's barometer in the natural food chain of many species of wildlife. An overpopulation of species that live on rabbits, such the lynx, coyote, and bobcat, is usually followed by a decline in the rabbit population, and vice versa. No one knows what controls this biological trigger.

Another interesting sidelight is that there is an ailment which can be called "rabbit starvation," although the early woodsmen and explorers, who often suffered from it, never knew what it was. The rabbit is not a perfect food, in that it lacks certain vitamins and minerals necessary to sustain human life. Lost in the woods, for example, if you tried to live off rabbit exclusively, no matter how you stuffed yourself with it, sooner or later you'd begin to waste away, lose strength, and finally die.

In 1881 the U.S. Consul General in Shanghai shipped twenty-eight ringnecked pheasants home to the Willamette Valley in Oregon. This exotic import created one of the country's finest game bird populations. Nearly ten million pheasants are bagged each year, and in some states such as South Dakota the pheasant season is a major industry.

The U.S. pheasant today, although resembling the original Chinese ringneck, is a mixture which includes the English and Mongolian pheasant. And, needless to say, is a superb hunting and eating bird.

Other imported exotics such as the chukar and Asian

partridges are also gaining ground rapidly in the United States.

Shot almost to extinction by market hunters in the 1920's, the wild duck and wild goose are now maintained precariously by agencies of three countries, with public funds and with contributions to Ducks Unlimited. About fifteen million wild ducks and one million geese are killed by hunters each year, of which the mallard, canvasback, and widgeon are the most plentiful. Most of the hunting today is confined to private clubs and to regulated public shooting areas.

Originally venison meant any game but today it is usually synonymous with deer meat, although quite properly it should include elk, moose, antelope, and reindeer.

The important thing to remember about any big game meat is to trim the fat away *completely*. It is too strong for domestic use and should be replaced with fat salt pork or suet. Wild venison, you will note, is not marbled like domestic beef, but is more grainy and muscled.

To lard venison after all the fat has been removed, pierce the meat with a skewer or long knife and push strips of chilled larding pork into the flesh, and wrap slices of larding pork around the meat and fasten with a string.

Andrew S. Landforce, wildlife management specialist at Oregon State University Extension Division, and one of the authors of several booklets on handling, butchering, and preparing big game and fish, has had long experience with his specialty, going back to boyhood days on the farm when venison was a staple.

In those days farmers and ranchers would as soon

eat one of their own children as butcher one of their own cows.

"In spite of what people say, venison is one of the finest eating of all meats—provided it's cooked right," Andy told me.

Part of his job involves traveling around the state putting on demonstrations with deer carcasses furnished by the Oregon State Game Commission, at 4-H clubs, community and Grange meetings, and sportsmen's groups.

One of his most memorable performances took place before a large crowd at the Warm Springs Indian Reservation where deer hunting is a year-around activity. During his demonstration Andy began to feel that he really did not have much audience contact, although the Indians gave him their rapt attention.

Finally, as he concluded, he walked to the edge of the platform and asked an Indian lady in the front row, who had been taking it all in stoically, how his method of boning deer differed from the old traditional Indian way.

"We did it the same way," she replied, "only we didn't spoil the meat."

That same night, at a social gathering, Andy politely asked an elderly man if he did much deer hunting on the reservation.

"No, we don't hunt deer," the tribesman said.

This seemed strange to Landforce, so he pressed the point.

"Oh, we kill a lot of deer," said the old man. "But we don't hunt. We put out a salt block and wait for them to hunt us."

The secret of enjoying delicious venison (meaning deer meat in this case) Landforce said, is to get rid of all the fat, butcher and store it properly, and then cook it right.

His book on boning out deer is useful also for commercial butchers, who are swamped with requests each fall by successful hunters to cut up their meat. Some state laws forbid hanging such game with the hide on in the same cooling and aging rooms with domestic meat—which creates a problem when you realize how much venison is brought home each year.

His method of boning, developed for amateurs, is one way out of the problem which now sees thousands of pounds of valuable meat spoiled or thrown away each fall.

VII

SOME FAVORITE RECIPES

Grilled Steelhead

Jim Conway, television's "Outdoor Sportsman," gave me this simple but superb recipe for western steelhead trout, which is really a seagoin' rainbow.

Clean, skin, and fillet the fish. Season with salt and pepper and brush with melted butter. Barbecue about six inches above hot coals. Turn occasionally, brushing top with butter each time. Cooking time is usually ten to fifteen minutes, depending on size of fish. When flesh pulls apart easily, it is done. Serve with tartar sauce and lemon.

Smoked Steelhead

Another recipe "borrowed" from Jim Conway, who "borrowed" it from Rogue River guide Bob Pruitt, is one that encourages larceny.

Clean fish and split to the backbone from vent or belly side, leaving the skin intact on the back. Open like a book, leaving both halves flat and secure fish in a frill.

Let a good campfire burn to embers. Place a layer of alder twigs with lots of leaves directly on the coals. As soon as you have a smoky fire, lay the fish flesh side down on the alder. The smoke will saturate the meat, and the leaves in a few moments will burn away.

Now turn the fish with its skin side down and lay

directly on the coals. Salt, pepper, and brush butter on flesh side. Soon the bottom will start to simmer as the heat from the coals penetrates the fish. Test frequently with knife or fork until done.

Eat right off the skin and you'll never forget its rare and delectable taste and smoky, outdoor flavor.

Deep-fried Steelhead

Jim Conway told me this was the only way he could get his family to eat fish, and it not only works on steelhead but any game fish.

Skin and fillet, removing rib bones and cut into one-inch chunks. Season with salt and pepper.

Mix a heavy batter of beer and buttermilk pancake flour. Dip pieces of fish in mix until completely covered and deep fry till brown.

That's all there is to it.

Tom McAllister, veteran outdoor editor of the *Oregon Journal*, and long a Dutch oven *aficionado*, remembers best these rare and delectable dishes:

Bill's Orgy

Billy Deeks, my hunting partner, called that evening by the Owyhee River with the Dutch oven between us, a "gastronomical orgy."

Now a leg, now a breast, we picked the disjointed pieces of five chukar partridge and eight mountain quail from the pot and tossed the bones in a sage fire heaped at our back for light and warmth.

Certainly, when a man has combined deer and chukar hunting into one long day of going over tumbled slopes and rims, he is famished.

But in the midst of the attack on the oven, Billy, who is built like a brick wall and has an incinerator appetite, waved a quail breast at me to punctuate his thoughts.

"They never ate like this in the Waldorf!"

Well, hardly, sitting cross-legged in the river sand with a community pot between us and fingers for eating with.

Our companion in this epicurean circle, George Skorney, didn't indulge himself in conversation. He just made noises of pleasure.

The recipe for that evening under the frowning ryholite spires and castellated cliffs of the Owyhee country:

Skinned and disjointed, the chukars and quail shot that afternoon in the spring creek draw behind camp were washed in the stream, then dredged with flour.

The birds were browned in butter in the Dutch oven, then removed and the oven filled with a couple of cans of sauerkraut. Then the pieces of bird were laid in the kraut bedding, and some water was added before setting the oven on the bed of coals.

The lid was placed on the oven and coals shoveled on top of the lid.

The sauerkraut keeps the flesh of the birds moist, so is ideal for baking them. And the taste blends admirably with the native flavor of the game.

McAllister's Pork Scallops

When you return to camp from a day's deer hunt on the Malheur breaks, the greatest virtue of a Dutch oven is that "instant dinner," which is then unearthed.

Stews and roasts are standbys, but the family favorite is scalloped potatoes and pork chops. I learned about this as a boy in Billy Berry's sheep camp in the Jackass Mountains and never forgot.

Slice enough raw potatoes to more than half fill the Dutch oven, and include some onion slices.

Before placing the potatoes and onions in the oven, brown a dozen pork chops and remove them, but leave the grease. Cut off some of the pork fat and leave several chunks of this in the bottom of the oven, too.

Then layer in the onion and potato slices, sprinkle with salt and flour. Nearly cover the potatoes with milk, until it can be seen through the top layer. Place the pork chops in a layer on top.

In the meantime the crew should have dug a hole for the oven and had hot coals ready to shovel into the bottom of the hole, and more to put on top of the lid. When all this is done, and the lid covered with coals, cover with dirt and tamp down firmly.

If this has been done in the morning, the Dutch oven may have cooled somewhat during the day. So when you remove it from the hole, pour some sour cream over the top of the chops and reheat them over the fire.

During this all-day cooking process, the chops have dripped and mingled their flavor all the way through the potatoes and onions.

The result is all the heavenly virtues, rolled into one pot—Dutch oven, that is.

APPENDIX

Building a Fire

You would think that building a fire outdoors would be the simplest chore in any camping experience, given a pocketful of matches, some combustible materials, and a little Boy Scout spirit. But, as the elephant said to the flea, there's more to it than meets the eye. In this era of the Population Explosion and the clamor for the last of the living and breathing space, open fires are not welcome and are frequently prohibited— especially in forested or grassland areas. Practically everywhere the cutting of standing timber is, with good reason, frowned upon.

Select a place for your campfire carefully, such as a spot protected from the wind, but close to water and on solid soil which contains no humus or organic materials. Scoop out a pit about two feet in diameter and a foot and a half deep. Line the pit with small rocks. Then scoop out a trough leading from the pit to a shallow depression about two or three feet away. With this arrangement, both above-ground and below-ground cooking can be accomplished.

Now cut your firewood from *dead* timber in pieces about a foot or so in length. The kind of firewood used has a great deal to do with the quality of outdoor cooking and the allowance made for cooking time. This, however, can only be determined by individual experience, and not out of cookbooks.

Softwoods burn quickly, often too quickly. Evergreens such as pine and fir are extremely resinous and burn with a pungent odor. Some woods pop and crackle, some smoke and leave lots of hot embers; others burn down to small ash. Oak, hickory, aspen, poplar, maple, alder, and other hardwoods are ideal for long-burning, fragrant, and relatively smokeless fires. In the Southwest, mesquite makes an excellent cooking fire.

Start your fire with a small wad of tinder under a pyramid of dry twigs, leaving air space for a good draft. If tinder is damp or hard to light, try placing a small stub of candle under it. Also pellets and tabs for starting fires are available from outfitters and sporting goods stores. Cooking fires should be no larger than necessary to do the job, and the actual cooking should not start until the fire has burned down to glowing coals. Alcohol in gelatin form is now available and is an excellent fire starter or even an emergency cooking fire.

Outdoor Fireplaces

An outdoor fireplace can be constructed easily and inexpensively in no time at all. First prepare the ground for a level base. Place a dozen or so cinder or pumice blocks as a base or platform. Lay more blocks around three sides to form the fire pit. A grill or wire rack can then be placed between the first and second layers of the walls.

That's all there is to it.

A fireplace can also be built in a few minutes' time with nothing but a supply of rocks. Stack the rocks to form three sides around a dug pit and lay a grill or wire mesh over it.

Two green logs will also serve as sides for a crude fireplace.

Sources of Supply

The standard cast ironware camp Dutch oven manufactured today comes in sizes from eight inches through sixteen inches in diameter. It is cast with three integral legs, and a flanged lid with handle. The capacity ranges from two quarts for the eight-inch size to twelve quarts for the sixteen-inch size. The cost ranges from $3.20 to $13.75. Weight ranges from seven pounds to thirty pounds for the large size.

The most popular size appears to be the twelve-inch, six-quart model, which is stocked by the National Supply Service of the Boy Scouts of America.

Two manufacturers are:

Lodge Manufacturing Co.
South Pittsburg, Tenn.   37380

Griswold Manufacturing Co.
Division of Randall Co.
P.O. Box 261
Sidney, Ohio   45365

The following firm distributes the new aluminum Dutch oven in a ten-inch and a twelve-inch size. The twelve-inch model weighs about seven pounds, compared with twelve pounds for ironware; and the ten-inch model weighs four pounds. The latter comes without legs and is designed to nest inside the larger model. A separate three-legged grill is supplied instead of legs for the ten-inch model.

Scott Foundry
3159 West 68th St.
Cleveland, Ohio

Other Sources

"A Cardboard Smokehouse," Fishery Leaflet 204, Fish & Wildlife Service, Washington, D.C.

"Curing of Fishery Products," Research Report No. 18, Supt. of Documents, 75¢.

"Home Preservation of Fishery Products," Fishery Leaflet 18, Fish & Wildlife Service.

"The Smoke Curing of Fish," Anderson & Pederson, Tech. Report No. 1, Washington State Department of Fisheries.

"Game Foods," Cooperative Extension Service Bulletin 790, Oregon State University.

"A Smokehouse for the Sportsman and Hobbyist," Cooperative Extension Service Bulletin 788, Oregon State University.

"How To Smoke Fish," Netcraft Co., 2144 Charleston Ave., Toledo, Ohio.

Mr. Phil Jensen, Luhr Jensen & Sons, Hood River, Oregon.

For powdered sourdough mixes and camp supplies:

The Ski Hut
1615 University Ave.
Berkeley, Calif.   94703

Recreation Equipment, Inc.
523 Pike Street
Seattle, Wash.   98101

Accessories for use with the camp Dutch oven could also include a small coal shovel, or trenching tool, for handling hot coals and for digging pits. Also useful would be a pothook for handling the lid and the oven. This can be an iron rod about 2 feet long with a hook on one end and a handle on the other. Instead of a solid rod, a stout wire with a hook on one end and a handle on the other could be used. This could be coiled up for convenience in packing and storage.

Handy Measures

1 pinch	=	$\frac{1}{8}$ tsp.
1 dash	=	same
3 tsps.	=	1 tbsp.
2 tbsps.	=	1 fluid oz.
4 tbsps.	=	$\frac{1}{4}$ cup
6 tbsps.	=	$\frac{3}{8}$ cup
8 tbsps.	=	$\frac{1}{2}$ cup
16 tbsps.	=	1 cup
No. 1 can	=	$1\frac{1}{3}$ cups
No. 2 can	=	$2\frac{1}{2}$ cups
No. 3 can	=	4 cups
No. 10 can	=	13 cups
1 lb. sugar	=	2 cups
1 lb. butter	=	2 cups
1 lb. cornmeal	=	3 cups
1 lb. beans	=	$2\frac{1}{2}$ cups
1 lb. flour	=	4 cups
1 lb. raisins	=	3 cups
1 lb. rice	=	2 cups

Cooking Measures

dash	less than $\frac{1}{8}$ teaspoon
3 teaspoons	1 tablespoon
4 tablespoons	$\frac{1}{4}$ cup
$5\frac{1}{3}$ tablespoons	$\frac{1}{3}$ cup
16 tablespoons	1 cup
1 cup	$\frac{1}{2}$ pint
2 cups	1 pint
2 pints	1 quart

4 quarts (liquid) .... 1 gallon
8 quarts (solid) .... 1 peck
4 pecks .... 1 bushel
16 ounces .... 1 pound
2 tablespoons butter .... 1 ounce
½ cup butter .... 1 stick or ¼ pound
2 cups butter .... 1 pound

Oven Temperatures

Slow oven	=	about 300° F.
Moderate oven	=	about 350° F.
Hot oven	=	about 400-450° F.

A pinch of flour in a pan inside a heating oven:

light brown in 5 minutes	=	slow
golden brown in 5 minutes	=	moderate
dark brown in 5 minutes	=	hot

Note: A longer cooking time is required at high altitudes:

0 to 3,000 feet	=	no change from sea level
3,000 to 4,000 feet	=	increase by 25° from sea level temp.
4,000 to 5,000 plus	=	increase by 50° from sea level temp.

Herb Chart

The addition of the right herb to the cooking pot can transform an ordinary dish into an inspiration. Exotic new flavors are possible through imaginative experimentation. But remember that with herbs, it's the light touch that makes the hit. Herbs should enhance, not overpower, natural food flavors. The rule is that too little is better than too much. Herbs lose flavor and aroma in time, so should be purchased in small amounts and replaced often. Store in dry places away from heat.

BASIL: Vegetable juices, soups; salads; venison, small game, birds, liver, stews, milk gravies, stuffings; halibut, mackerel, shellfish; most vegetables.

CHERVIL: Soups, cream and others; green and cream salads; beef, chicken, stews, stuffings; fish sauces; peas, carrots, spinach.

CHIVE: Appetizers, soup toppings; many salads and dressings; topping for meats; all fish; potatoes, lima beans.

DILL: Spreads and dips, tomato juice, soups; seafood and green salads, dressings; chops, veal, creamed chicken, gravy; all fish and shellfish, fish sauces; herb butter; brussels sprouts, green beans, carrots, beets, peas, cauliflower, tomatoes, potatoes.

MARJORAM: Tomato juice, soups; green, chicken, and seafood salads; meats, poultry, game, stews, stuffings; all fish, lobster, creamed crab; asparagus, broccoli, brussels sprouts, carrots, beans, peas, potatoes.

MINT: Fruit juices, bean, pea soup; coleslaw, tossed and fruit salads; lamb, veal sauces; all fish, fish sauces, peas.

OREGANO: Vegetable juices, bean, chowder, tomato soups; green, seafood, potato salads; pork, veal, lamb, chicken, duck, stews, stuffings; all fish and shellfish, fish sauces, herb butter; broccoli, onions, peas, potatoes, spinach, squash.

PARSLEY: Canapés, dips, spreads, soups; almost all

salads; all meats; all fish, shellfish, fish sauces, herb butter; all vegetables.

ROSEMARY: Appetizers, pea, chicken, turtle soups; green, fruit and meat salads; meats, poultry, game, stews, stuffings, gravy; all shellfish and fish; green beans, cauliflower, spinach, potatoes, eggplant, turnips.

SAGE: Some appetizers, soups; cream or cottage cheese, salad dressing; meats, poultry game, stews, stuffings, gravy; all fish and shellfish, fish stuffings; brussels sprouts, green beans, cabbage, eggplant, stewed tomatoes, turnips.

SAVORY: Vegetable juices, vegetable soups; green, tomato, potato, egg salads, coleslaw; meats, poultry, game, stews, stuffings, gravy; all baked or broiled fish; asparagus, brussels sprouts, peas, green beans, cucumbers, squash, cabbage, cauliflower.

TARRAGON: Cheese dips and spreads, vegetable juices, soups, chowder; seafood, chicken salad, aspic; meats, poultry; all fish and shellfish, fish sauces; asparagus, broccoli, green beans, cauliflower, beets, spinach, cabbage, tomatoes.

THYME: Cheese and seafood dips and spreads; soups, chowder; seafood and chicken salads, aspics; meats, poultry, game, stuffing; all fish and shellfish, fish sauces; asparagus, peas, green beans, spinach, carrots, tomatoes, beets, potatoes, onions.

INDEX TO RECIPES